African American Homeownership Initiative

Volume 1

Eric Lawrence Frazier MBA

Your Trusted Advisor in Business and Wealth

African American Homeownership Initiative
Volume 1

Dedication

To every African American family who has dreamed of homeownership, faced barriers, and yet continues to push forward. This book is for you — and for the generations to come who will walk through doors that once stood closed.

ERIC LAWRENCE FRAZIER, MBA BUSINESS BOOKS

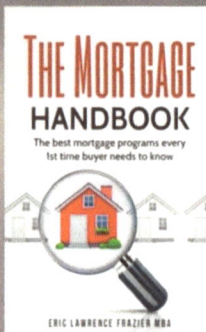

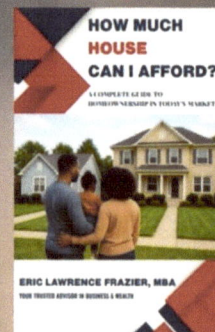

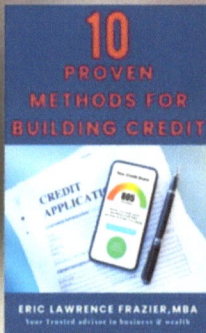

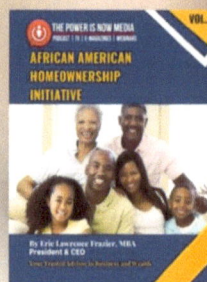

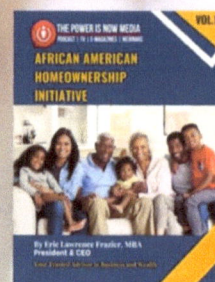

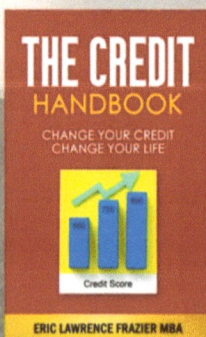

ERIC LAWRENCE FRAZIER, MBA POETRY BOOKS

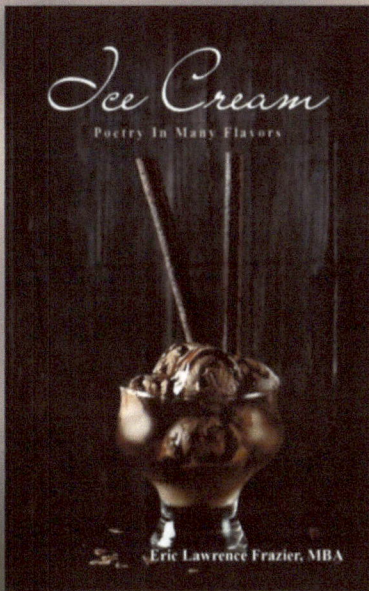

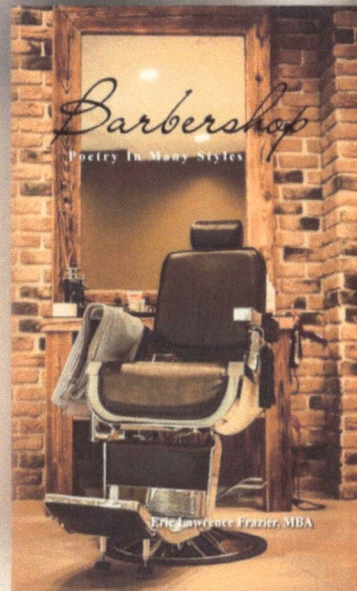

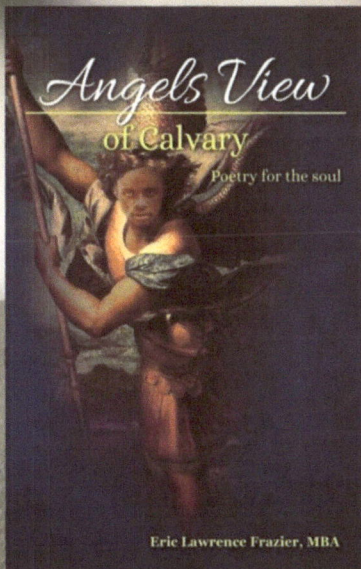

Ice Cream
Poetry In Many Flavors

Eric Lawrence Frazier, MBA

Barbershop
Poetry In Many Styles

Eric Lawrence Frazier, MBA

Angels View
of Calvary

Poetry for the soul

Eric Lawrence Frazier, MBA

TABLE OF CONTENTS

Preface

This book was born out of both frustration and determination. Frustration that, after decades of civil rights victories and policy efforts, the Black homeownership gap remains stubbornly wide. Determination because change is not only possible but necessary.

The African American Homeownership Initiative lays out the evidence, history, and contemporary realities of housing inequality in America. More importantly, it offers strategies — practical, systemic, and community-driven — to break cycles of exclusion and create sustainable opportunities for wealth building.

The chapters that follow will take you through the key barriers: financial literacy gaps, wage and wealth disparities, mortgage discrimination, and limited access to information. They also introduce solutions built on the principles of **Depower, Demystify, and Develop.**

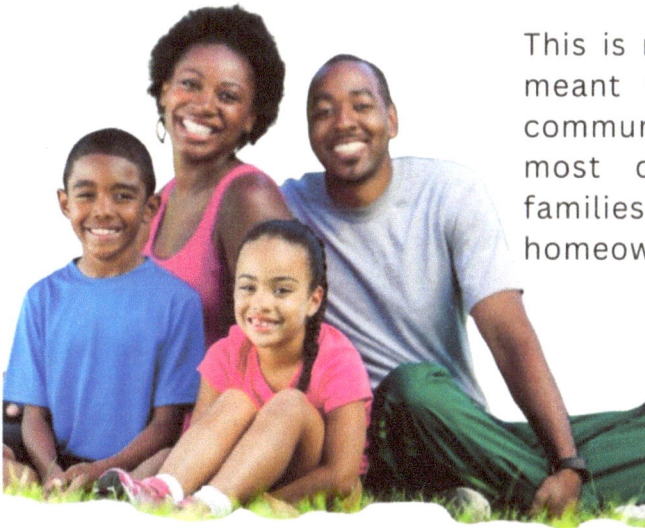

This is not just an academic text. It is meant to be used by policymakers, community leaders, educators, and most of all, by African American families navigating the path toward homeownership.

Acknowledgments

This book would not have been possible without the encouragement, contributions, and dedication of many.

I wish to thank:

- The research teams. housing advocates, and organizations whose tireless work provided the foundation for much of the data and insight shared here.

- My colleagues and collaborators who reviewed drafts, offered critical feedback, and strengthened the vision behind this initiative.

- Finally, my family and community, whose unwavering belief in the transformative power of homeownership has been my deepest motivation.

To all of you — this work belongs as much to you as it does to me.

Homeownership has been the cornerstone of any strong economy. Research shows homeownership is tied to multiple social and economic benefits to an individual. It has also been viewed as the fastest way to build generational wealth. The Federal Reserve's data in 2019 showed that the net worth of a homeowner was $255,000 while that of a renter was $6,300.

Based on net worth, it pays to be a homeowner. Still, other measurable benefits are attributed to homeownership, such as better educational performance, high civic engagement, volunteerism, better health care, and lower crime rates.

Why the Disparity in Homeownership?

1. Poor Financial Literacy

There is a documented link between financial literacy and financial stability among African Americans. The lack of financial literacy finds its roots in slavery and unequal opportunities in education which is why Brown vs. Board of Education was passed by the Supreme Court. The unfortunate reality is that the legacy still lingers and requires outreach.

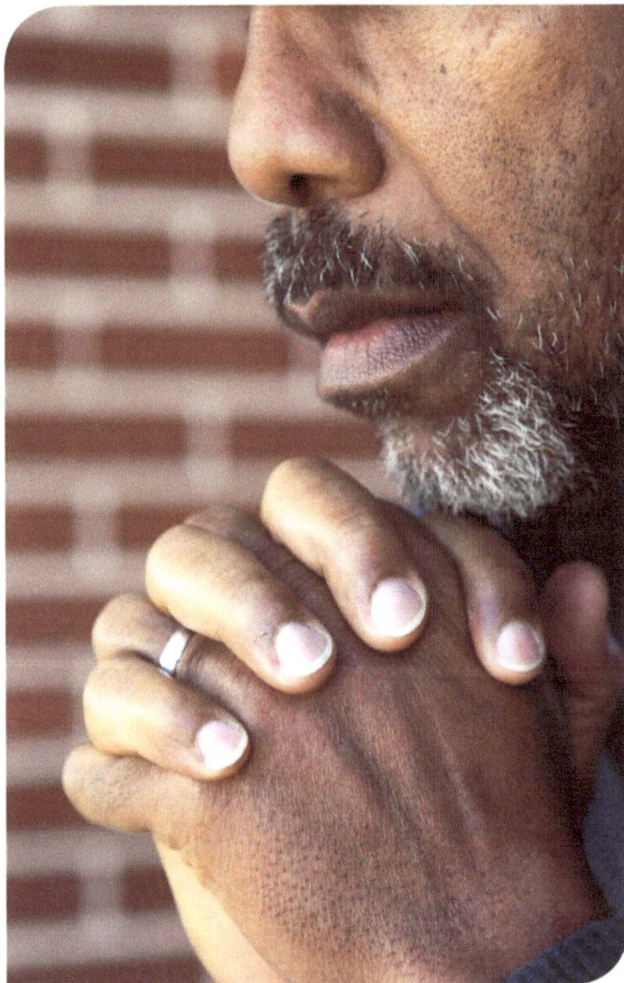

2. Legacy of Wage Disparity and Income Discrimination

There is long-established research that documents the wage disparity and income discrimination between African Americans, whites, and other minorities. You cannot afford a home if you cannot make enough money. Wage disparity exists not because of job qualifications. It exists because of racism and being denied the opportunity to make more money.

3. Home Loan Discrimination

Since the beginning of FHA/VA and the securitization of loans, African Americans have been victims of discrimination and redlining. They are denied at a significantly higher rate than whites for home loans. There have been numerous lawsuits filed and won by the attorney generals and many laws on the books because of racism in lending and real estate.

4. Limited Information and Outreach to African Americans

The revenue and ROI associated with DPA and CCA loans are very limited and borrower-paid. Very few banks participate in the programs because of that, and very few, if any, spend money to advertise these programs in the media. In addition, there are even fewer opportunities sponsored by banks and nonbanks to educate African Americans about homeownership and mortgage programs because the costs to do so further diminishes their ROI.

Unfortunately, many people have missed out on the benefits of homeownership due to social status or ethnic affiliations. Minority communities are behind the national average. Working the homeownership benefits backward; this disparity in ownership can be attributed to poor educational and career performance and low net worth for themselves and their family.

This cycle of accepting a lie and the ability for minorities to build wealth and realize the community benefits of homeownership can stop today. It starts with discovering the truth about African American Homeownership.

African American Homeownership Initiative

The Power Is Now Media Inc. is based in Riverside, California. California's Black homeownership rate today is lower now than it was in the 1960s when it was completely legal to discriminate against Black homebuyers. California's history of housing discrimination against African Americans is one significant reason that the rate of homeownership is lowest among all minority groups. African Americans were specifically targeted and denied access to housing because of exclusionary housing policies and practices beginning with the first Governor of California, Peter Hardeman Burnett. He supported the abolishment of slavery but openly stated and ran on a platform that he did not want African Americans in California. California adopted every tactic in the book for Government-sponsored redlining, racist covenants restricting the sale of property to whites only, and predatory lending. African Americans' homeownership rate in California today reflects discrimination that has resulted in the lost opportunity to build generational wealth.

The African American Homeownership Initiative aims to address the significant gap between African Americans and other ethnic groups and provide information, education, and support to make a difference and close the gap. The most significant barrier to homeownership is the down payment. The second barrier would be financial literacy and education about down payment assistance and HUD counseling opportunities to address credit and money management. These issues transcend race and ethnicity but have had a disparate impact on African Americans because of systematic racism at the highest level of Government and the private sector, especially regarding housing, going back as far as slavery. African American Homeownership Initiative is a multicultural homeownership initiative to help all people of color, race, ethnicity, sexual orientation, and gender build wealth through homeownership. Our initial focus will be on the African American community (AFAHI) but we are also launching the same initiative in the Asian American community (AACHI), the Latino American community (LAHI), the LGBTQ community (LGBTQHI), and Low- to Moderate-Income communities (LMIHI).

Our Strategy – Depower, Demystify and Develop

Our first strategy is to impact the African American community by depowering discrimination, defending Fair Housing, demystifying homeownership, and developing low- to moderate-income and first-time homebuyers.

Depowering Discrimination

Discrimination is not going away anytime soon. It is woven into the fabric of this country since the beginning of slavery. Even after the emancipation proclamation discrimination increased as the African American community tried to exercise their new freedom. It would make amendments to the constitution and the Supreme Court to protect and enable African Americans to enjoy some degree of freedom and prosperity in the United States. So to depower discrimination is to reduce the power of discrimination. We will never be able to strip the power of discrimination from people whose desire is to discriminate and treat others differently because of the color of their skin, race, natural origin, gender, or sexual orientation.

We will depower discrimination through education and collaboration in multi-cultural organizations, which seek to bring people together and make homeownership a reality for everyone. We will depower discrimination through legislation and lobbying in Washington DC to change policies and lending guidelines that make it more difficult for minorities and people of color to access credit and housing.

We will depower discrimination by working with banking and real estate organizations that seek to hire diverse real estate professionals and mortgage professionals to serve the communities of color in which they have branches or offices.

Demystify Homeownership

We will demystify homeownership by providing online seminars about the homebuying process mortgage programs, budgeting, credit, and the requirements of purchasing a home and maintaining and keeping the home once it has been purchased.

To demystify anything is to make it clearer and simpler and easier to understand. The goal is not only to make it easier and simpler to understand but also to make the information accessible anytime, anywhere, and on-demand. As a media company, we are uniquely equipped to provide access to this information in the way that the borrower chooses to receive it.

Develop Homeowners

We will develop homeowners through strategic alliances with housing finance agencies, churches, nonprofit organizations, and community organizations that currently serve the needs of their respective communities through education and support. We will be their strategic partner to provide and disseminate information and create opportunities for their constituents to learn about homeownership, obtain loan approval, identify real estate professionals, and even find a home to purchase for a seller who desires to support the initiative. Homeowners are not born, they are developed through education, mentoring, and preparation.

Our Second Strategy – To Be a Homeownership Resource

We want to impact all other communities regardless of color or disability, gender, sexual orientation, and national origin. We want The Power Is Now Media to be the resource for real estate professionals and minority consumers nationwide to make the dream of homeownership a reality for everyone.

We will start with the African American community first because The Power Is Now Media is African American-owned and operated. The founder is a leader in the African American community and has established networks in business, education, banking, and community organizations.

Secondly, limited human and financial resources prohibit us from going wide so we must go deep where we already have roots and build from there. At the same time because of our established relationships with other minority real estate trade associations and community organizations, we will work with them in tandem as we serve and prioritize the African American community.

Thirdly, the African American experience is a unique experience. Unlike many other people in America, our experience is deep-rooted in our great pain and tragedy in slavery. The pain has continued since our emancipation by government-sponsored racism, black codes, Jim Crow, and other community lead and systemic racism you can imagine. Discriminations and racism have set the African community back in every aspect of Black life in America and especially in the area of homeownership.

The Plight of African American Homeownership

Since the emancipation of African Americans from slavery in 1863, every barrier you can imagine, both private and government-sponsored discrimination has blocked their efforts to build wealth in real estate and to fully participate in the American Dream of financial independence and freedom. African Americans celebrate their independence from slavery on June 19th, 1865—2.5 years after the Emancipation Proclamation because four million slaves were not told that they were free until then. Slavery begins in 1619 in the tobacco fields of Virginia. African Americans were still slaves on the 4th of July 1776, the birth of American Independence, and continued to be slaves for an additional 157 years. It would take many acts of congress and federal intervention to secure the rights and protection of African Americans and still do to this very day. The history below outlines the long and painful journey to freedom and opportunity:

1. **1865:** The 13th Amendment abolished slavery and set African Americans free to die. No protection, no reparation, no citizenship, no land, no money. Many died.
2. **1867:** The 14th Amendment granted African Americans citizenship but it was second-class citizenship, and they were not able to participate fully as free citizens.
3. **1869:** The 15th Amendment gave African Americans the right to vote but barriers came up to stop them at every turn.
4. **1875:** The Civil Rights Act barred discrimination in public accommodations which led to the segregation of everything, but you risked your life entering a white-only establishment.
5. **1964:** The Civil Rights Act 99 years later barred discrimination in employment, public facilities, and schools and yet discrimination continued.
6. **1965:** The Voting Rights Act – suspended the use of literacy tests and voter disqualification devices for five years. So threats and intimidation were employed to keep them from voting.
7. **1968:** The Fair Housing Act – prohibited discrimination in the sale of or rental of approximately 80% of housing. It wasn't until the 70s that even realtor associations allowed Blacks to represent buyers and sellers and racism was still practiced.

[1] https://www.npr.org/2017/05/03/526655831/a-forgotten-history-of-how-the-u-s-government-segregated-america
[2] https://www.history.com/news/housing-segregation-new-deal-program
[3] https://www.history.com/news/black-soldiers-world-war-ii-discrimination

From 1950 to 1980 the total Black population in American urban centers increased from 6.1 to 15.3 million. Whites moved out of the cities into the suburbs and took the employment opportunities with them. The Federal Housing Administration, which was established in 1934, furthered the segregation efforts by refusing to insure mortgages in and near African American neighborhoods—a policy known as "redlining." At the same time, the FHA was subsidizing builders who were mass-producing entire subdivisions[1] for whites—with the requirement that none of the homes be sold to African-Americans[2].

The Great Depression of the late 1920s and early 1930s delivered a gut punch to the average American. By 1933, a quarter of Americans were out of work, the national average income had slumped to less than half of what it had been a few years earlier and more than one million Americans faced foreclosure on their homes.

The Federal Housing Administration (FHA) through the Housing Act of 1934 was an integral component of the New Deal legislation. It was created for the purpose of salvaging the home building and finance industries that had collapsed during the Great Depression.

The FHA had a manual that explicitly said that "It was risky to make mortgage loans in predominantly Black areas," explains Richard D. Kahlenberg, a senior fellow at The Century Foundation who has written about housing segregation in the United States. "And so, as a result, the federal subsidy for homeownership went almost entirely to white people."[3] The financial assistance program not only limited recipients to white Americans, but it also established and then reinforced housing segregation in the United States, effectively drawing lines between white and Black neighborhoods that would persist for generations.

World War II exposed a glaring paradox within the United States Armed Forces. Although more than 1 million African Americans served in the war to defeat Nazism and fascism, they did so in segregated units and came home to segregated communities. After World War II officially ended on September 2, 1945, Black soldiers returned home to the United States facing violent white mobs of those who resented African Americans in uniform and perceived them as a threat to the social order of Jim Crow. In addition to racial violence, Black soldiers were often denied benefits guaranteed under the G.I. Bill, the sweeping legislation that provided tuition assistance, job placement, and home and business loans to veterans.

The Federal Housing Administration and the Veterans Administration financed more than $120 billion worth of new housing between 1934 and 1962, but less than 2% of this real estate was available to nonwhite families—and most of that small amount was located in segregated communities. In other words, for almost three decades the U.S. government backed $120 billion worth of home loans and 98% (!) of those loans went to whites[5].

Today African American incomes on average are about 60 percent of average white incomes. But African American wealth is about 5 percent of white wealth. Most middle-class families in this country gain their wealth from the equity

[3] https://talktostambrose.wordpress.com/2009/10/12/aint-so-simple-housing-privilege-and-wealth-inequality/
[4] https://www.npr.org/2017/05/03/526655831/a-forgotten-history-of-how-the-u-s-government-segregated-america
[5] https://www.npr.org/2017/05/03/526655831/a-forgotten-history-of-how-the-u-s-government-segregated-america
[6] https://www.urban.org/urban-wire/these-five-facts-reveal-current-crisis-black-homeownership

they have in their homes. So, this enormous difference between a 60 percent income ratio and a 5 percent wealth ratio is almost entirely attributable to the federal housing policy implemented through the 20th-century[6]. African American families that were prohibited from buying homes in the suburbs in the 1940s and '50s and even into the '60s, by the Federal Housing Administration, gained none of the equity appreciation that whites gained.[7]

The State of Black Homeownership

Unfortunately, since the Civil Rights Act of 1962 and the Fair Housing Act of 1968, the rate of homeownership has not improved for Africans. The African American rate of homeownership is the lowest of all ethnic groups and has been for a while. According to the U.S. Census Bureau Quarterly Residential Vacancies and Homeownership Rate for the Third Quarter of 2021 Report, released July 27th, 2021, the homeownership rate in the U.S. is 65.6 percent overall. The rate among whites is 74.2%, Asians 58.7%, Hispanics 47.5%, and African Americans 44.6%. According to Urban

Year/Quarter	Homeownership Rates (percent)										
	United States		Non-Hispanic White Alone		Black Alone		All Other Races				Hispanic (of any race)	
							Total[a]		Asian, Native, Hawaiian and Pacific Islander Alone			
	Rate	MOE[b]	Rate	MOE[b]	Rate	MOE[b]	Rate	MOE[b]	Rate	MOE[b]	Rate	MOE[b]
2021												
Second Quarter	65.4	0.5	74.2	0.4	44.6	0.9	56.2	1.1	58.7	1.3	47.5	0.9
First Quarter	65.6	0.5	73.8	0.4	45.1	0.9	57.1	1.1	59.6	1.3	49.3	0.9
2020												
Fourth Quarter	65.8	0.5	74.5	0.4	44.1	0.9	56.3	1.1	59.5	1.3	49.1	0.9
Third Quarter	67.4	0.5	75.8	0.4	46.4	0.9	58.0	1.1	61.0	1.3	50.9	0.9
Second Quarter	67.9	0.5	76.0	0.4	47.0	0.9	59.3	1.1	61.4	1.3	51.4	0.9
First Quarter	65.3	0.5	73.7	0.4	44.0	0.9	55.9	1.1	59.1	1.3	48.9	0.9
2019												
Fourth Quarter	65.1	0.5	73.7	0.4	44.0	0.9	55.7	1.1	57.6	1.3	48.1	0.9
Third Quarter	64.8	0.5	73.4	0.4	42.7	0.9	56.0	1.1	58.5	1.3	47.8	0.9
Second Quarter	64.1	0.5	73.1	0.4	40.6	0.9	55.0	1.1	57.7	1.3	46.6	0.9
First Quarter	64.2	0.5	73.2	0.4	41.1	0.9	53.9	1.1	56.9	1.3	47.4	0.9
2018												
Fourth Quarter	64.8	0.5	73.6	0.4	42.9	0.9	55.6	1.1	58.1	1.3	46.9	0.9
Third Quarter	64.4	0.5	73.1	0.4	41.7	0.9	56.6	1.1	58.2	1.3	46.3	0.9
Second Quarter	64.3	0.5	72.9	0.4	41.6	0.9	55.7	1.1	58.0	1.3	46.6	1.0
First Quarter	64.2	0.5	72.4	0.4	42.2	0.9	54.8	1.1	57.3	1.4	48.4	1.0
2017												
Fourth Quarter	64.2	0.5	72.7	0.4	42.1	0.9	55.4	1.1	58.2	1.4	46.6	1.0
Third Quarter	63.9	0.5	72.5	0.4	42.0	0.9	54.7	1.2	57.1	1.4	46.1	1.0
Second Quarter	63.7	0.5	72.2	0.4	42.3	0.9	54.3	1.2	56.5	1.4	45.5	1.0
First Quarter	63.6	0.5	71.8	0.4	42.7	0.9	53.6	1.1	56.8	1.4	46.6	1.0

[a]Includes people who reported Asian, Native Hawaiian or Other Pacific Islander, or American Indian or Alaska Native regardless of whether they reported any other race, as well as all other combinations of two or more races.
[b]A margin of error is a measure of an estimate's variability. The larger the margin of error in relation to the size of the estimate, the less reliable the estimate. This number, when added to and subtracted from the estimate, forms the 90 percent confidence interval.
Source: U.S. Census Bureau, Current Population Survey/Housing Vacancy Survey, July 27, 2021

Wire Race and Ethnicity Black[8] homeownership is in crisis. Although homeownership rates for other racial groups have largely recovered since the 2008 housing crisis, Black homeownership continues to decline, recently hitting an all-time low in the first quarter of 2019.
https://www.census. gov/housing/hvs/files/ currenthvspress.pdf.

Homeownership builds household wealth, intergenerational wealth, and economic mobility provides a hedge against inflation and improves civic engagement and voting.

According to Urban Wire Race and Ethnicity Data Talk,[9] there are five supporting facts that we are in a crisis in Black homeownership.[10]

1. The current 30-percentage-point gap between Black and white homeownership is larger than it was in 1968 when housing discrimination was legal.
2. If the Black homeownership rate were the same today as it was in 2000, America would have 770,000 additional Black homeowners
3. Homeownership is lower for Black college graduates than for white high school dropouts.

[9] https://www.urban.org/events/black-homeownership-gap-research-trends-and-why-growing-gap-matters.
[10] https://www.urban.org/urban-wire/these-five-facts-reveal-current-crisis-black-homeownership.
[11] https://www.jchs.harvard.edu/son-2020-homeownership-gap.

4. Black borrowers are less likely to meet the traditional credit standards necessary to qualify for a mortgage.
5. Seventeen percent of the Black-white homeownership gap can't be explained by identifiable factors.

According to the Joint Center for Housing Studies at Harvard University, the graph[11] below shows that African Americans are losing ground. There is no plan of action by the Government that has been approved by Congress to make a difference in the rate of homeownership. Also, there is no plan in the leadership of the African American community to address the problem. As the standard of living increases, education and incomes increase we are not seeing an increase in homeownership.

Wealth Inequality

The Great Recession of 2007–2009 triggered a sharp, prolonged decline in the wealth of American families, and an already large wealth gap between white households and Black and Hispanic households widened further in its immediate aftermath. But the racial and ethnic wealth gap has evolved differently for families at different income levels, according to the Federal Reserve Board's Survey of Consumer Finances.

In 2016, the median wealth of all U.S. households was $97,300, up 16% from 2013 but well below the median wealth before the recession began in late 2007 ($139,700 in 2016). In 2016, the median wealth of white households was $171,000. That's 10 times the wealth of Black households ($17,100)—a larger gap than

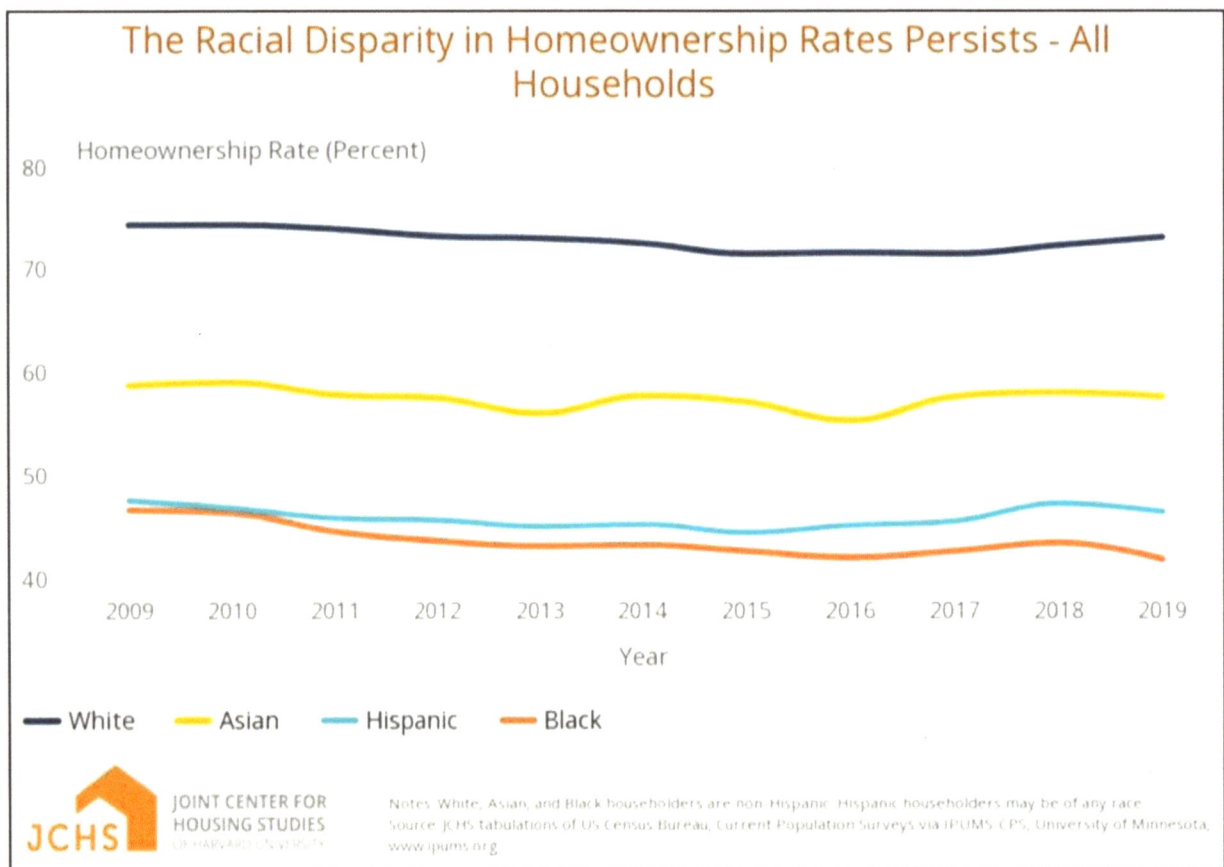

The Racial Disparity in Homeownership Rates Persists - All Households

Homeownership Rate (Percent)

Year

White Asian Hispanic Black

JCHS JOINT CENTER FOR HOUSING STUDIES OF HARVARD UNIVERSITY

Notes: White, Asian, and Black householders are non-Hispanic; Hispanic householders may be of any race. Source: JCHS tabulations of US Census Bureau, Current Population Surveys via IPUMS-CPS, University of Minnesota, www.ipums.org

[12] https://www.pewresearch.org/fact-tank/2017/11/01/how-wealth-inequality-has-changed-in-the-u-s-since-the-great-recession-by-race-ethnicity-and-income/.

in 2007—and eight times that of Hispanic households ($20,600), about the same gap as in 2007. (Asians and other racial groups are not separately identified in the Survey of Consumer Finances data. Figure 1.) [12]

Figure 1: Net worth by race/ethnicity, 2016 survey

Thousands of 2016 dollars

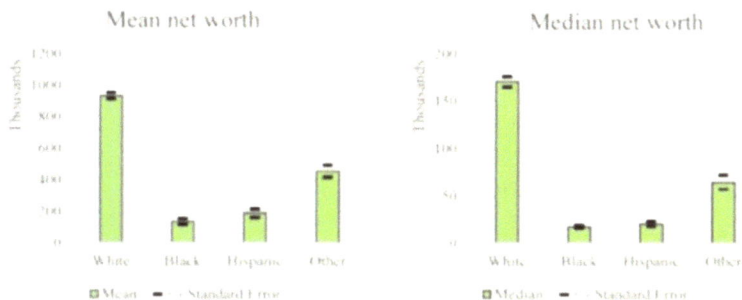

Source: Federal Reserve Board, Survey of Consumer Finances

Accessible version

In 2016, lower-income white households had a net worth of $22,900, compared with only $5,000 for Black households and $7,900 for Hispanic households.

The income correlates to differences in homeownership rates among families—49% for lower-income whites, versus 31% for lower-income Blacks and 30% for lower-income Hispanics.

25% of white households are in the lower-income tier, compared with about 50% each of Black and Hispanic households.

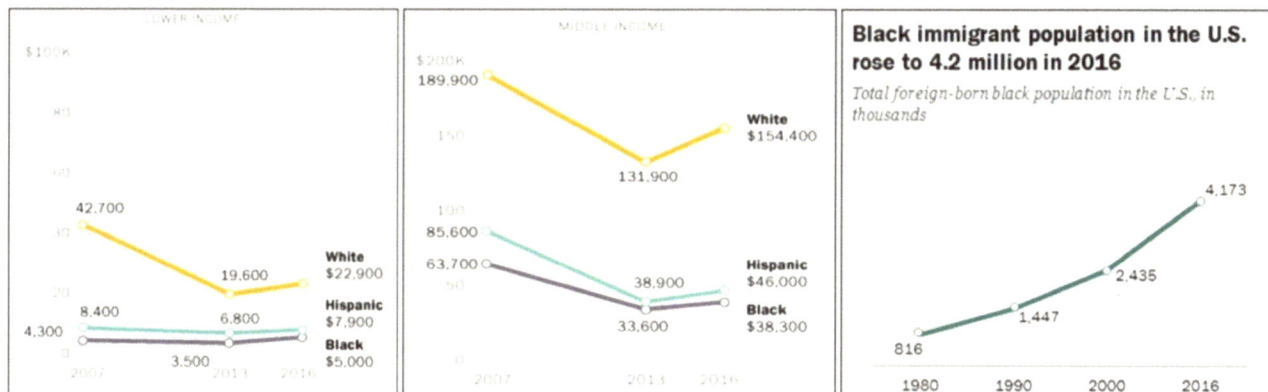

Therefore low levels of wealth are much more prevalent among Black and Hispanic households than among white households.

Black Immigrants

There were 4.2 million Black immigrants living in the U.S. in 2016, up from just 816,000 in 1980, according to a Pew Research Center analysis of U.S. Census Bureau data. The number of Black immigrants living in the country has risen 71%. Approximately one in ten Blacks (9%) living in the U.S. are foreign-born, up from 3% in 1980. (Immigrants make up 10% of the Black population in the March 2016 Current Population Survey.[13]

[13] https://www.pewresearch.org/fact-tank/2018/01/24/key-facts-about-black-immigrants-in-the-u-s/

The Power Is Now Media Black Homeownership Wealth Research

The following are summaries of research reports about homeownership in the United States and the impact of not owning homes is having on African Americans and people of color:

CALIFORNIA ASSOCIATION OF REALTORS
Report on California Housing Affordability by Ethnicity
https://www.car.org/en/aboutus/mediacenter/newsreleases/2021releases/haibyethnicity.

Published: February 2021

Summary

- Housing affordability for Black California households is half that of whites, illustrating persistent wide homeownership gap and wealth disparities, C.A.R. reports
- Less than one in five Black California households could afford to purchase the $659,380 statewide median-priced home in 2020, compared to two in five white California households who could afford to purchase the same median-priced home.
- At an affordability index of 20 percent, the affordability gap was similarly wide for Latinx households.
- A minimum annual income of $122,800 was needed to make monthly payments of $3,070, including principal, interest, and taxes on a 30-year fixed-rate mortgage at a 3.30 percent interest rate.

Introduction

Housing affordability for Black California families is half that of white families, according to the California Association of Realtors (C.A.R), demonstrating that considerable homeownership disparities and wealth inequalities persist. In 2020, just one out of every five Black California households will be able to buy the state's median-priced house of $659,380, compared to two out of every five white California households.

With a 20 percent affordability index, Latinx households faced a huge cost gap. A minimum annual income of $122,800 was necessary to make monthly payments of $3,070, including principal, interest, and taxes, on a 30-year fixed-rate mortgage with a 3.30 percent interest rate. C.A.R. showed that fewer than half of Black families made enough money to purchase a home, highlighting the homeownership gap and economic discrepancy for people of color, women, persons with disabilities, indigenous peoples, and LGBTQ people.

In 2020, 19% of Black homebuyers in California could afford a median-priced existing single-family house, compared to 38% of white households. Housing affordability was also a problem for Latinx families, with just 20% earning the minimum income necessary to purchase a median-priced home. Asians had the most affordable housing, with 43 percent of buyers able to afford the median-priced house in 2020. According to the Census Bureau's American Community Survey, the 2019 homeownership rate in California was 63.2 percent for whites, 60.2 percent for Asians, 44.1 percent for Latins, and 36.8 percent for Blacks.

C.A.R. is taking many steps to combat housing discrimination, including sponsoring many Fair Housing and Equity laws, such as:

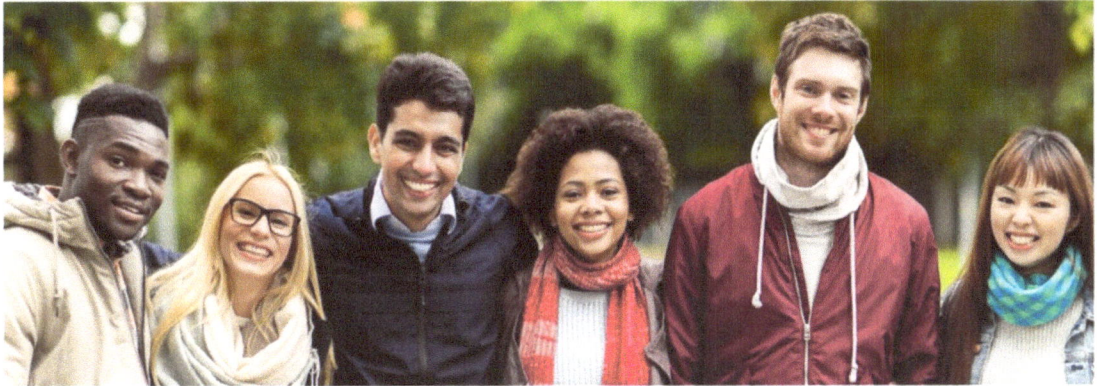

- Requiring California real estate professionals to complete implicit bias training.
- Removing discriminatory language from property records.
- Prohibiting discrimination against low-income residents.
- Repealing Article 34 of the California Constitution.

The C.A.R. Housing Affordability Index (HAI) measures the percentage of California households that can afford to purchase a median-priced single-family house. C.A.R. also publishes affordability indices for individual localities and counties throughout the state. The index is recognized as the most fundamental indication of housing well-being for homebuyers. To purchase a $659,380 statewide median-priced existing single-family home in 2020, a minimum annual income of $122,800 was necessary. The monthly payment, including taxes and insurance, for a 30-year fixed-rate loan with a 20% down payment and an effective composite interest rate of 3.30 percent would be $3,070. Whites had a median income of $94,390 in 2020, compared to $107,100 for Asians, $65,510 for Latinx, and $56,820 for Blacks.

The affordability gap is very obvious in inexpensive places like San Francisco, where a median-priced home of $1,650,000 was only affordable for 8% of Black families, 15% of Latinx households, and 22% of Asian families, compared to 35% of white families. In 2020, compared to 62 percent of white families in California, 42 percent of Black families in the United States could afford a $299,900 median-priced house, which required a minimum annual income of $55,600 and monthly payments of $1,390.

With a 27 percent differential in affordability between Black and white households in San Francisco County in 2020, it was the greatest of the major places for which C.A.R. assesses affordability by ethnicity. Even in relatively inexpensive areas such as Fresno and Sacramento counties, the affordability difference between Black and white families remained large, at 23% and 22%, respectively. Santa Clara County has the largest affordability gap for Latinx families (21 percent), followed by San Francisco, San Mateo, and Los Angeles counties (all at 20 percent). With an affordability index of 8%, San Francisco County was the least affordable for Black families, while San Bernardino County was the most affordable, with a 46 percent affordability index.

In 2020, Santa Clara County was the least affordable county for Latinx homeowners, while San Bernardino County was the most affordable, at 54%. Orange County was the costliest for white families, with just 29% of families earning the required minimum wage, while Fresno was the most affordable, with 61%. For more than 110 years, the California Association of Realtors has been a leader in California real estate. It is one of the largest state trade associations in the nation, with over 200,000 members dedicated to the advancement of real estate professionals. C.A.R.'s headquarters are in Los Angeles.

NATIONAL ASSOCIATION OF REALTORS
Report on Black Homeownership

https://www.nar.realtor/sites/default/files/
documents/2021-snapshot-of-race-and-home-
buyers-in-america-02-18-2021.pdf.

Published: February 2021

Summary

- NAR finds Black homebuyers more than twice as likely to have student loan debt and be rejected for mortgage loans than white homebuyers.
- The U.S. homeownership rate was 64.2% in 2019. At 69.8%, the rate for non-Hispanic white Americans exceeds the national rate. However, the Black homeownership rate—42%—represents a Black-white homeownership gap of almost 30%. The homeownership rates for Asian Americans and Hispanic Americans are 60.7% and 48.1%, respectively.
- Black households—43%—are more than twice as likely as white households—21%—to have student loan debt, with a median student loan debt for Black households of $40,000 compared to $30,000 for white households.
- Black applicants were rejected for mortgage loans at a rate 2.5 times greater than white applicants—10% vs. 4%, respectively. Nationwide, 43% of Black households can afford to buy the typical home compared to 63% of white households.

Introduction

The years 2020–2021 will always be glued in our memories because of the pandemic that caused severe economic turmoil the world over. Many households and businesses had to adopt various strategies to survive and those that did not die a sudden death. Millions of people lost their jobs due to the shutdown orders and ever since millions more haven't been able to recover their jobs even after the country made a partial comeback to a state of normalcy. While the pandemic was indiscriminate, affecting everyone across the board, the impacts and the consequences especially with job losses have been so disproportionate with a high number of losses being seen among the African American communities and the Hispanic/Latino communities. Ultimately, we expect a recovery of the economy to some degree later this year as the COVID-19 vaccines become available to many more Americans.

While we were grappling with the impacts of COVID-19 across most frontiers of both our personal and professional lives, something interesting was happening. The housing market was booming, weathering through the storm caused by the pandemic. It came as a surprise because many experts concurred that people would be warier, holding back any major purchases. But contrary to that popular opinion, home sales activity rose to the highest peak in 14 years in 2020 contributing

significantly to the recovery of the U.S. economy.

Housing and homeownership have always been the cornerstone of any strong economy, but accepting its importance, research has been consistently showing that homeownership is associated with multiple economic and social benefits to the individual. In fact, homeownership has always been viewed as the fastest way to build generational wealth. The Federal Reserve's data in 2019 showed that the net worth of a homeowner was $255,000 while that of a renter was $6,300 which basically points out that the net worth of a homeowner is 40 times that of a renter. In addition to the tangible benefits attributed to homeownership, it also brings so many substantial benefits in terms of societal gains to the family, communities, and the country at large. Research has also shown that owning a home contributes to better educational performance, high civic engagement and volunteerism, better health care, and lower crime rates.

Nevertheless, not so many people or families have been fortunate enough to be counted in the basket of homeownership, which means so many miss opportunities and the benefits of owning a home. Indeed, looking at homeownership through the prism of social status and ethnic affiliations, there are sizable differences in the homeownership rates where we have the minority communities lagging behind the national average. This ultimately translates into poor performance and low net worth for the minority communities because homeownership is tied directly into a person's or a family's net worth.

Homeownership Trends in the Past Decade

According to a report by NAR, 2021 Snapshot of Race and Home Buying in America, Americans are less likely to own their own homes compared to 10 years earlier. And while the homeownership rate has been consistently rising since 2015, it is yet to surpass the record made in 2009 where the rate was 66.0%. More importantly, there were more people becoming homeowners in 2019 than a year earlier. The homeownership rate increased by a low margin of 0.2% which translates to nearly 1 million more homeowners!

Looking at these numbers, it is easy to draw the conclusion that the country's housing industry is doing better than most and that the people fare well financially. The homeownership rate for white Americans has always been consistently ticking at 70 percent since 2017.

At the same time, the homeownership rate for African Americans has been consistently 30 percentage points lower at 41 percent in 2017 and 45.1 in the first quarter of 2021. Compared to other minority communities in the country, the rate of homeownership for the Blacks has been stagnant, not doing well and not falling so far back. In the past decade, the homeownership rate rose for only Asians, reaching a new high of 60.7 percent in 2019 up by 1.2 percent. Since 2009, the rate of homeownership for the African American community has been declining to suggest that the community never fully recovered from the effects of the financial crisis.

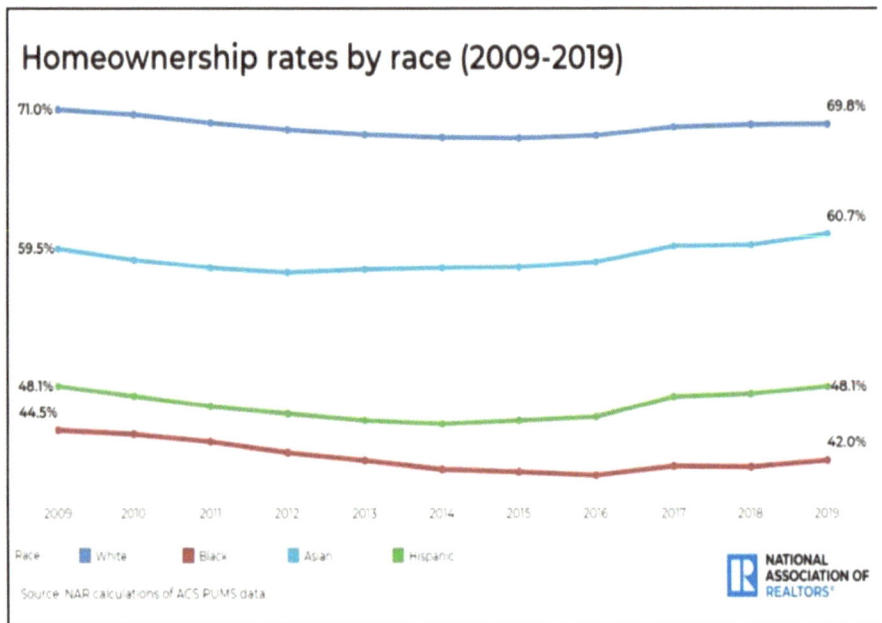

Homeownership rates by race (2009-2019)

Source: NAR calculations of ACS PUMS data

According to NAR, going by the state, high rates of homeownership for the Black community in 2019 were recorded in Puerto Rico at 70 percent, and South Carolina at 52 percent while the lowest rates were recorded in North Dakota at 5 percent, Wyoming at 18 percent and Montana at 20 percent. To put it into perspective, the homeownership rate for the African American community in the country varied from 5 percent to 70 percent and among the 52 states, just 18 states had a rate higher than 42.0 percent.

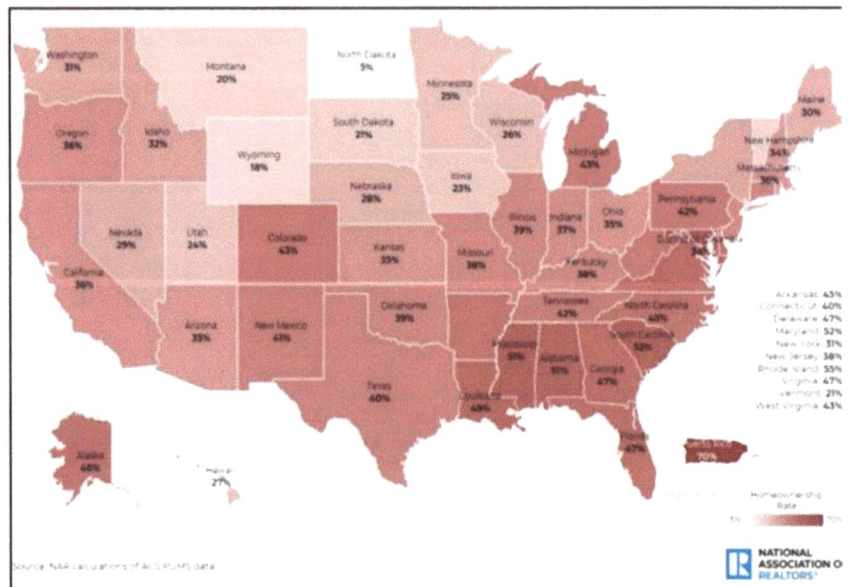

Source: NAR calculations of ACS PUMS data

Housing Affordability by Race

Almost in all areas, the housing demand shot up surpassing the supply by a greater margin and with the increased demand, the home prices also increased quite significantly. Consequently, this has crippled affordability all across the country. To be more specific, the inventory continues to dwindle, reaching new record lows. But there is a reason for this. In the past decade, there haven't been significant construction projects going on in the country, thus, a constrained supply of new homes. In December alone, due to increased buyer demand, the inventory of existing homes for sale dropped significantly and to date, that was the lowest it has been.

The likely scenario that will occur in the next couple of months, and even might go into the next year is that home prices will keep on increasing. In fact, there is enough evidence that shows that home prices have steadily risen for the last decade. In December, home prices were up 13 percent than a year earlier and 40 percent more than five years ago.

Looking at the affordability index by race, nationally, 43 percent of African Americans can afford the average home compared to 63 percent of non-Hispanic whites. It is the lowest given that 71 percent of Asians and 54 percent of Hispanics can comfortably afford the average home. It is important to also highlight that the affordability of a given home is directly tied to the location of the property. In addition to that, it is also important to note that the high prices of homes in most areas are eroding the ability of most people to afford these homes, making it more difficult for most people to accomplish their dream of homeownership.

Going by the states, African Americans are able to comfortably afford a home in South Dakota (75 percent) and Alaska (73 percent) while just 20 percent are able to buy in the District of Columbia, Wyoming, and Hawaii.

Affordability
Share of households that can afford to buy the typical home

	White	Black	Asian	Hispanics
Alabama	74%	55%	73%	63%
Alaska	64%	73%	58%	47%
Arizona	57%	47%	66%	50%
Arkansas	74%	56%	86%	76%
California	33%	20%	44%	20%
Colorado	48%	30%	48%	32%
Connecticut	64%	42%	74%	42%
Delaware	65%	46%	79%	47%
District of Columbia	56%	14%	39%	36%
Florida	58%	43%	65%	50%
Georgia	70%	53%	74%	60%
Hawaii	24%	18%	27%	17%
Idaho	57%	48%	57%	49%
Illinois	70%	45%	76%	62%
Indiana	76%	53%	74%	69%
Iowa	76%	51%	72%	67%
Kansas	76%	61%	76%	70%
Kentucky	70%	59%	79%	67%
Louisiana	70%	48%	70%	57%
Maine	64%	45%	73%	81%
Maryland	64%	49%	70%	53%
Massachusetts	51%	31%	58%	30%
Michigan	74%	53%	80%	68%
Minnesota	68%	40%	70%	55%
Mississippi	77%	56%	84%	66%
Missouri	72%	56%	76%	69%
Montana	55%	32%	40%	47%
Nebraska	74%	60%	69%	62%
Nevada	50%	32%	53%	47%
New Hampshire	62%	57%	76%	61%
New Jersey	59%	37%	74%	42%
New Mexico	65%	58%	72%	58%
New York	55%	37%	54%	40%
North Carolina	68%	49%	77%	57%
North Dakota	69%	39%	26%	61%
Ohio	76%	52%	83%	63%
Oklahoma	74%	56%	71%	67%
Oregon	46%	22%	55%	38%
Pennsylvania	70%	47%	72%	52%
Rhode Island	61%	38%	70%	39%
South Carolina	73%	49%	73%	62%
South Dakota	71%	75%	69%	72%
Tennessee	67%	52%	79%	55%
Texas	69%	54%	77%	59%
Utah	55%	27%	51%	41%
Vermont	62%	61%	74%	70%
Virginia	62%	44%	71%	55%
Washington	48%	32%	63%	33%
West Virginia	72%	56%	84%	76%
Wisconsin	71%	43%	74%	60%
Wyoming	65%	16%	40%	62%

Source: NAR calculations of ACS PUMS data

NATIONAL ASSOCIATION OF REALTORS

Financing Options for the African Americans Financing remains at the pinnacle of enabling African Americans to achieve their dream of homeownership. Research shows that African Americans and Latinos face extra challenges when trying to get a mortgage. The NAR's Profile of Homebuyers and Sellers shows that 10 percent of Black homebuyers and 6 percent of Latinos were denied a mortgage, compared to only 4 percent of the non-Hispanic whites and Asians. Dominant among the reasons why most Blacks and Hispanics were denied a mortgage was a low DTI, but a majority of the African Americans cited that they were denied a mortgage because of a low credit score.

According to data from ACS PUMS, the majority of African Americans are more likely to finance their home purchase. In fact, nationally, in 2019, 76 percent of white homeowners financed their home purchase compared to 81 percent of African Americans. At the same time, it is to be noted that most non-Hispanic whites earned more than African Americans wherein the median income of white homebuyers was $90,000 compared to the $70,000 of a Black homebuyer.

Where most Black home buyers financed their home purchase

Share of Black home buyers who financed their home purchase in 2019

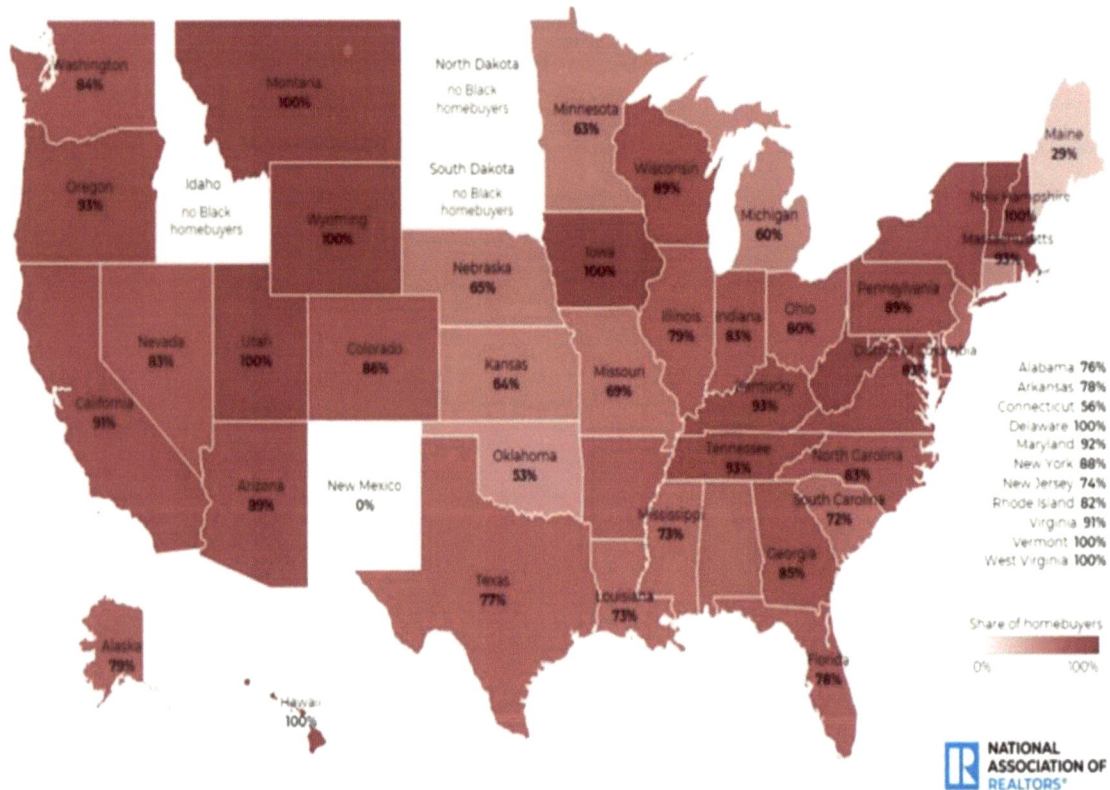

The map shows where most African Americans financed their home purchase. In the following nine states, African American buyers were able to finance their home purchase in 2019; Delaware, Hawaii, Iowa, Montana, New Hampshire, Utah, Vermont, West Virginia, and Wyoming.

https://www.nar.realtor/sites/default/files/documents/2021-snapshot-of-race-and-home-buyers-in-america-02-18-2021.pdf.

Where most Black home buyers financed their home purchase

Share of Black home buyers who financed their home purchase in 2019

Washington 84%
Montana 100%
North Dakota no Black homebuyers
Minnesota 63%
Maine 29%
Oregon 93%
Idaho no Black homebuyers
Wyoming 100%
South Dakota no Black homebuyers
Wisconsin 89%
Michigan 60%
New Hampshire 100%
Massachusetts 33%
Nebraska 65%
Iowa 100%
Nevada 83%
Utah 100%
Colorado 86%
Kansas 64%
Missouri 69%
Illinois 79%
Indiana 83%
Ohio 80%
Pennsylvania 89%
California 91%
Kentucky 93%
Arizona 89%
New Mexico 0%
Oklahoma 53%
Tennessee 93%
North Carolina 83%
South Carolina 72%
Mississippi 73%
Georgia 85%
Texas 77%
Louisiana 73%
Alaska 79%
Hawaii 100%
Florida 78%

Alabama 76%
Arkansas 78%
Connecticut 56%
Delaware 100%
Maryland 92%
New York 88%
New Jersey 74%
Rhode Island 82%
Virginia 91%
Vermont 100%
West Virginia 100%

Share of homebuyers
0%　　100%

NATIONAL ASSOCIATION OF REALTORS®

Source: NAR calculations of ACS PUMS data

2021 Snapshot of Race and Home Buying in America

15

JOINT CENTER FOR HOUSING STUDIES OF HARVARD UNIVERSITY
A Report On the State of the Nation's Housing for Black Americans

https://www.jchs.harvard.edu/sites/default/files/reports/files/Harvard_JCHS_The_State_of_the_Nations_Housing_2020_Report_Revised_120720.pdf.

Published: November 2020

Summary

On Housing Markets:

- Mortgage rates dropped in 2020 to the lowest rates since 1989 while credit conditions tightened, limiting access to mortgages. This contributed to an increase in a monthly median sale price that reached $281,200 in the first half of 2020, a 3.3 percent rise from 2019.
- The rental supply grew by 7.5 million units from 2004 to 2019. Most new units were single-family rentals or in buildings with at least 20 apartments—apartment stock that is typically more expensive than those in smaller multifamily structures.

On Housing Demand and Household Formation:

- Renter households headed by a person of color made up about three-quarters of growth from 2004 to 2019. Growth in homeownership rates among households of color was also high, though disparities in homeownership rates remain.

- In 2019, the homeownership rate for white households was 73.3 percent and 42.8 percent for Black households, the largest gap since 1983.
- The share of adults younger than 35 heading their households increased for the first time in 10 years.

On Housing Affordability:

- In 2019, 20.4 million renters were cost-burdened, spending more than 30 percent of their incomes on housing. Black, Latinx, and Asian households experienced cost burdens at higher rates than white households.
- Of households earning less than $25,000, 62 percent paid more than half their income on housing.
- In 2019, the number of people experiencing homelessness increased by 15,000, bringing the total to nearly 568,000.
- Black people, Native Americans, Alaskan Natives, and the Latinx population experienced rates of homelessness disproportionately larger than their total population in the United States.

On Race or Ethnicity and Neighborhoods:

- Two-thirds of households with low incomes headed by people of color live in high-poverty areas, compared with one-third of white people with low incomes.
- Thirty-eight percent of Black people with incomes above the federal poverty level live in high-poverty areas, more than three times the share of white people with the same incomes.

Introduction

The COVID-19 epidemic, social upheaval fueled by long-standing racial inequality, and the severe effects of climate change plagued the nation for most of 2020. Low borrowing rates and steady growth in certain industries have boosted homebuying and the wider economy, but things have become worse for many families. Indeed, the country's inability to meet its long-stated aim of providing a good home in an appropriate environment for everybody has never been more evident, especially in the shortage of cheap rental housing and uneven access to purchase.

Decreasing Renters' Affordability

The COVID-19 pandemic's economic consequences have exacerbated the rental affordability dilemma. According to the Census Bureau's Household Pulse Survey for late September, renters earning less than $25,000 a year were far more likely to report lost job income during the March closure. Indeed, compared to 41% of all families, more than half of the lowest-income renters (52%) lost earnings over this time. Not unexpectedly, one in every five tenants earning less than $25,000 reported they were overdue on their rent, compared to 15% of all renters and just 7% of those earning more than $75,000.

Those earning $25,000 to $49,999 a year also suffered, with 53% losing their jobs and 16% falling behind on their rent.

Renter families of color have disproportionately felt the pandemic's effects. Even before the COVID-19 epidemic, the cost-burdened portions of Black and Hispanic renters were already more than ten percentage points higher than white renters, at 54 percent and 52 percent, respectively. However, the difference between white and Asian tenants was just 0.3 percentage points. Also, many of these families have experienced income losses as a result of the economic downturn. Consequently, by late September, 23% of Black, 20% of Hispanic, and 19% of Asian tenants were behind on their payments, about double the 10% rate of white renters.

Many tenants could stay afloat because of federal assistance granted via the CARES Act, which included increased unemployment benefits, stimulus payments, and funding for state and local relief operations. The entire economy has improved, with the unemployment rate falling from 14.7 percent in April to 6.9 percent in October. Still, without extra government help, many families who have skipped rent payments may be unable to pay their back rents. Additional government spending would help tenants stay in their homes and give much-needed assistance to property owners.

Landlords are feeling the heat as well, with so many renters in financial hardship. Although weekly surveys by the National Multifamily Housing Council reveal that rent delinquencies in professionally managed buildings averaged slightly under 10% by the 20th of each month from May to October; the full effect of the economic crisis on owners is yet unclear.

Even yet, collections at properties that aren't generally handled by a professional are substantially smaller. During the final two weeks of September, 17 percent of renters in single-family homes and 14 percent of renters in smaller multifamily buildings were late on rent, compared to 11 percent of tenants in larger apartment complexes, according to the Household Pulse Survey.

Household Age and Diversity

With people of color accounting for such a substantial part of the household increase, income disparity has substantial implications for the strength of future housing demand. Over the last five years, families of color have made up almost three out of every four new families. From 2014 to 2019, Hispanic households accounted for 36% of the household increase (400,000 each year), bringing their total households to 14%. In 2019, Black households accounted for 17% of the total increase (190,000 each year) and made up 12% of all households. Another 15% (165,000 each year) of the rises came from Asian homes, bringing their total households to 5%.

In 2019, they accounted for 23% of total household growth (260,000 per year) and two-thirds of all households. Households of color make up a larger proportion of younger households, accounting for little over 90% of those under 35. Over the last five years, the number of Black, Hispanic, Asian and other minority households aged 35–64 has grown sufficiently to counteract the 2 million reductions in white families in this age range, with Hispanic families accounting for most of this rise. Diversity is gradually expanding within the 65-and-up age group, with the white percentage falling from 80% to 78% between 2014 and 2019.

Even though the return of household formations among the vast millennial generation has increased the number of younger-adult families in the United States over the last five years, the age distribution of U.S.

households continues to migrate higher. The baby-boom generation (born 1946–1964) gradually replaces the considerably smaller group that came before them in the 65-and-up age bracket. Consequently, the number of households aged 65 and above is growing faster than any other age group, both in terms of total households and as a percentage of all families. Indeed, although the number of families under 45 climbed by one million between 2014 and 2019, the number of families 65 and over climbed by roughly a million per year, raising the ratio of older families from 24 percent to 26 percent.

Meanwhile, the younger half of the baby boomers are entering the 55–64 age bracket. Given that this is still the largest 10-year cohort of U.S. households, the younger boomers will continue to support growth in the number of households aged 65 and over shortly. Still, the population 75 and over, which is expected to grow by 48 percent in 2020–2030, will see the fastest growth over the next decade.

NATIONAL ASSOCIATION OF HISPANIC REAL ESTATE PROFESSIONALS (NAHREP)
The 2020 State of Hispanic Homeownership Report

https://nahrep.org/shhr/

nahrep

- Latinos will continue to lead in homeownership growth. Between now and 2040, it's projected that 16.1 million new households will be formed, all of which will come from communities of color. Of those, 8.6 million will be Latino, 4.8 million will be Asian (or other) and 3.3 million will be Black.
- Nearly one in three Latinos rely on FHA financing.
- Over the next 20 years, 70% of new homeowners will be Latino, adding an additional 4.8 million net new homeowners.

Introduction

The National Association of Hispanic Real Estate Professionals (NAHREP) released its 2020 State of Hispanic Homeownership Report, and the data provide the first glimpse at ownership statistics encompassing the impact of COVID-related economic challenges. The main takeaway is that mortgage relief initiatives such as forbearance have apparently prevented any backslide in ownership rates thus far—at least for this demographic group. Hispanics were more likely than other ethnicities to have suffered job loss during the pandemic, so this is an encouraging indicator.

Summary

- The 2020 Hispanic homeownership rate is 48–49%. This is the only demographic in the U.S. to continuously increase their rate of homeownership for each of the last six years.
- Over 54% of the Hispanic population in Illinois are homeowners.
- There are 8.3 million mortgage-ready Latinos under the age of 45.

Impact of the Pandemic on the Latino Community

Just like other demographics, the COVID-19 pandemic has threatened and affected the progress the Latino community has made in bridging the wealth gap. The Latino community has undoubtedly been affected by the pandemic with the infection rate as high as three times more than that of the non-Hispanic whites. Data shows that Hispanics 55 years and below are 6 times more likely to die from the COVID-19 infection than non-Hispanic whites. Economically, the Latinos are also simultaneously more likely to have been considered essential workers (21 percent) during mandatory stay-at-home orders and experience loss or reduction of income. Latinos are twice as likely as non-Hispanic white workers to be unemployed due to the pandemic. Only 28.9 percent of Latinos are able to work from home, compared to 48.7 percent for non-Hispanic white workers, and many have depleted their savings since the start of the pandemic. The outsized health and economic impacts of the pandemic will unfortunately slow Latino household wealth growth in the years to come. Nevertheless, Latinos remain optimistic.

Sustained Homeownership Growth Despite Pandemic

Despite job losses from the COVID-19 pandemic, record-low housing inventory, and a restrictive credit environment, Latinos increased their homeownership rate for the sixth consecutive year. Record-low interest rates and an overwhelming desire to purchase a home during the pandemic resulted in historic levels of demand for homeownership. Latinos are the only demographic in the U.S. to increase their rate of homeownership for each of the past six years.

The number of Latinos aging into prime homebuying years remains the biggest catalyst for homeownership growth. With a median age of 29.8, Latinos are almost 14 years younger than the non-Hispanic white population. In 2020, nearly half (43.6 percent) of Latino homebuyers were under the age of 34, compared to 37.3 percent of the general population. Today, nearly one in three Latinos is currently in the prime homebuying years of 25–44.

Latinos Are Forging the Future of the Housing Market

In the ten years leading up to the pandemic, Latinos accounted for over 50 percent of homeownership growth in the U.S.2 This trend is expected to accelerate for the next 20 years. According to projections made by Urban Institute, all future homeownership growth will come from non-white households, with Latinos accounting for 70 percent of homeownership growth over the next 20 years.

While Latinos have made headway in homeownership gains over the past decade, growth has not been equal across the country or Latino subgroups. Latino homeowners, like the Latino electorate, are not monolithic. Latinos in the U.S. stem from over 20 Latin American countries with different races, socioeconomic, and migration backgrounds. While the 2019 Hispanic homeownership rate was 47.5, the Afro-Latino homeownership rate was 41.8 percent. And, Latinos of Guatemalan, Dominican, and Honduran descent had a homeownership rate below 32 percent. Over half of U.S. states and territories have a homeownership rate above the national average with Wyoming and South Carolina experiencing the greatest growth in Hispanic homeowners. New York, Massachusetts, and Connecticut states with high-cost markets have the lowest Hispanic homeownership rates.

Record-Low Housing Inventory

The lack of affordable housing inventory remains the number one barrier to advancing sustainable Hispanic homeownership. When looking at the top ten markets where Latinos purchased the most homes in 2019, housing inventory dropped an average of 50.6 percent in suburban neighborhoods and 26.6 percent in urban neighborhoods. Homeowner vacancy rates in 2020 dropped for the seventh consecutive year to 1.0 percent, the lowest rate ever recorded by the U.S. Census. Latinos have a median credit score of 668, a median debt-to-income ratio of 41 percent, and purchase homes with a median down payment of 3.5 percent—all borrower profiles that make them particularly vulnerable to underwriting changes. According to the Mortgage Bankers Association (MBA), credit availability in 2020 was the most restrictive credit access environment in six years.

Opportunities for Growth

There are 8.3 million Latinos under the age of 45 with the credit characteristics to potentially qualify for a mortgage. These "mortgage-ready" Latinos create substantial opportunities for additional homeownership growth over the next few years. While Latinos tend to be concentrated in high-cost areas, the growth is taking place in nontraditional markets as Latinos are willing to relocate to areas rich with housing and employment opportunities. In 2019, the top two fastest-growing markets for Latino homebuyers were Durham/Chapel Hill, North Carolina, and Boise, Idaho, both with a year-over-year growth rate of more than 40 percent.

Conclusion

In 2020, a once-in-a-century pandemic devastated families, crushed the U.S. economy, and caused record unemployment and business closures. Latinos, in particular, were harshly impacted by the effects of the pandemic, from both a health and economic standpoint. However, supported by historically low interest rates, and robust consumer demand, the real estate market had a surprisingly strong year. The youth of the Latino community also helped overcome many of the pandemic-induced economic setbacks, driving household growth and increasing the Latino homeownership rate for the sixth consecutive year; the only demographic with six straight years of growth. While a large gap in homeownership rates continues to exist between Latinos and the general population, the gap is getting smaller. In the ten years leading up to the pandemic, Latinos accounted for more than 50 percent of the net homeownership growth in the U.S. Looking forward there are substantial headwinds such as access to credit and record-low housing inventory that can slow homeownership growth for Latinos and the overall population. While the pandemic has taught us that the future is not guaranteed, it has also illustrated how the housing market fares so goes the U.S. economy, and no demographic is playing a more central role in America's housing economy than Latino-Americans.

URBAN INSTITUTE &
THE NATIONAL COMMUNITY REINVESTMENT
COALITION
Reducing the Racial Homeownership Gap

https://www.urban.org/policy-centers/housing-finance-policy-center/projects/reducing-racial-homeownership-gap.

https://ncrc.org/60-black-homeownership-a-radical-goal-for-black-wealth-development/.

Published: March 2021

Summary

- A decline over the past 20 years left the Black homeownership rate at 42% in 2018, as low as it was in 1970. The rate for white homeownership was 73% in that same year.
- A 20%–30% gap between Black/white homeownership rates has persisted for more than 100 years, despite Black homeownership increases in the mid-1900s.
- African Americans go into greater debt for less valuable homes and receive less of a return on homeownership than whites.
- If holding the current rates of Black homeownership formation and loss constant, then it would require approximately 165,000 additional new Black homeowners annually over the next 20 years to get to 60% Black homeownership by 2040.
- Bold new approaches to housing finance and investment in community development are required to get to a 60% homeownership rate for African Americans.
- Even getting to a record-level Black homeownership rate of 60% will not bridge the Black and white wealth divide. Additional bold programs like baby bonds, full employment, and reparations are needed to close the Black/white wealth divide in the foreseeable future.
- Black populations with moderate incomes in geographic areas with affordable housing and low Black homeownership rates offer strong opportunities to increase African American homeownership.

Introduction

Data from a report by Urban Institute show that today, the homeownership gap between the non-Hispanic whites and the African American population in the United States is bigger than it was more than half a century ago when it was still legal to segregate people on the basis of color, religion and ethnic affiliation.

In the 1960s, the rate of homeownership between the African Americans and the non-Hispanic whites was a "not-so-large" margin of 27 percentage points, standing at 38 percent. Today, more than 50 years later, the rate has grown wider. After the passing of the Fair Housing Act of 1968, it was automatic that minority communities in America, especially the Black community would start seeing significant gains in many fronts of life, given the fact that homeownership is an integral part of wealth building, but the gains made in the last three decades were proactively erased after 2000. It would seem that forces in the housing industry aligned themselves strategically to reduce the Black homeownership rate.

The Housing Crisis of 2008–2010

This is one event that took the African American community far back, and even before the community fully recovered from this blow, the COVID-19 hit, destroying the numerous efforts by the community to build itself back up again. At the height of the 2008–2010 recession, many African Americans bought their homes at a higher interest rate than any other community, that is the non-Hispanic whites and Asian communities. Ultimately, this meant that African American buyers were disproportionately the victims of a predatory 'cartel' that offered subprime loans even to the people who were well able to afford prime loans at the time. It doesn't stop there; the African Americans who were lucky at the time to have bought their first home, the 'industry' aggressively solicited for unsafe refinance products. Consequently, these actions culminated in the deterioration of equity for the African American community and fueled a foreclosure crisis.

(i) Subprime Lending Practices against the Black Community

It is not a new phenomenon; it has been there before, and it still is despite promises of protecting the vulnerable communities. Unscrupulous lending and lenders dominated the housing boom of the 2000s. This led to having spurred significant damages to the people who fell prey in terms of social costs as many were misled into accepting the loans with inferior properties subject to the mortgage products that they had qualified for. While much of the evidence of predatory lending is anecdotal and primarily analyzes differential loan terms of a broad group of borrowers,

there is compelling evidence during the height of the housing boom, ten years before the financial crisis, Black homeowners and buyers were subjected to unfair lending practices. One report, the Loan Product Steering in Mortgage Markets, finds that many borrowers were charged 40-60 bps high APR and were 2 percent less likely to default compared to similar borrowers who were not steered into such loans. Strong evidence points to the fact a vast majority of African Americans were subjected to excessive fees, high-interest rates, prepayment penalties, and clauses that barred them from seeking judicial redress for such actions. While at the time steering potential borrowers to such loans were not necessarily nefarious, especially where the loan product could benefit a person who wouldn't qualify for a prime loan, it had adverse consequences if there was direct exploitation by steering people to particularly loan products that they were overqualified for.

(ii) Since the housing crisis of 2008-10, the tight lending and credit environment has disproportionately affected the Black and Latino communities in the United States. Consequently, these communities have been forced to find other means of 'survival' oftentimes opting for higher-priced homes since they cannot fully take advantage of the low home prices and low interest rates that followed the financial crisis of 2008-10. This meant that a huge number of well-qualified individuals from these communities missed out on wealth-building opportunities through homeownership. Today, credit and lending remain constrained while home prices shoot up beyond their pre-crisis peak, which further means that more African Americans and other minorities have limited access to affordable housing options.

Negating Wealth-Building

Opportunities for African Americans Post the Financial Crisis

Looking back to the crisis that was the 2008–2010 crisis, on average it is safe to say that African Americans did not benefit as much as the non-Hispanic whites from the recovery post the recession. Consequently, the African American rate of homeownership has since dramatically decreased more than 2 percentage points from 2000 to 2010 and after 2010, it fell further by a wide margin of 5 basis points. The decline in the rate of homeownership for the Black community threatens to further the racial inequality for years to come and for most families, homeownership remains an integral part of their wealth-building story. The disparate rates of wealth and homeownership for the African American population are a symbiotic issue that is likely to persist, leaving the African American community behind in the building of intergenerational wealth.

One of the sure ways vital to the fight against inequality is increased African American homeownership. Even with this knowledge, it is still surprising that there hasn't been any real progress in increasing the Black homeownership rates for most part of the 60 years that have passed, and in addition, a persistent lack of action in bridging the gap between the African Americans and the Non-Hispanic whites for the last 100 years. The continued effort to delay and derail African American homeownership is not new, but it needs a renewed sense of urgency. It is alarming that the African American rate of homeownership has been steadily declining from 2004's peak of 49 percent. The fact is the financial crisis of 2008 was never the trigger for the decline in homeownership for the Black community. There is enough evidence that points out to the fact that the past 15 years have seen the most dramatic decline in African American homeownership rates of any racial or ethnic group in the country. It is also a fact that today, the average African American homeowner owes more in mortgage debt than a non-Hispanic white owes on a house with less value. To put this in perspective, the average first home of an African American buyer is valued at $127,000, they also average $90,000 in mortgage debt. Comparing these numbers to those of an average non-Hispanic white homeowner, while their average home values at $139,000, they average $75,000 in mortgage debt. What this means is that, for a property that is valued less, the average first-time homebuyer in the African American community will go into greater debt, which ultimately weakens their return on investment for the property.

Early Trends in African American Homeownership

To understand where the community is coming from, we have to go back in time to a place where the Black lost it! In the 1930s, right after the great depression, the federal government sought to strengthen homeownership rates through the establishment of the Home Owners' Loan Act of 1933, which was accompanied by the creation of the Home Owners Loan Corporation (HOLC), which resulted in more than $3 billion in mortgage financing. There is enough documentation that shows the history of HOLC's discriminatory and disparate neighborhood desirability rating system whereby the predominantly white neighborhoods were perceived as the most desirable and would be outlined in city maps with green. You can even imagine the condition the 'undesirable' community was already living in. Most of these communities were marked as hazardous with down infrastructure and were usually outlined in red. To think that the Federal

Housing Administration was an institution that would step in to promote fairness would be outwardly wrong! In fact, the FHA enabled, ensured, and supported lending and went further to support development in the green zones—the predominantly white neighborhoods—leaving others with no development whatsoever. The injustice then was unbearable! Coupled with the slavery and Jim Crow laws, the housing policies then contributed largely to the unequal homeownership landscape. A decade later, in 1940, the African American homeownership rate was nearly half of the white homeownership rate, standing at 22.8 percent.

You would think that the decades that followed would see a decline in the Black homeownership rates, but contrary to that, despite the discriminatory policies Black homeownership rates rose dramatically between the years 1940 and 1960, recording an increase of 15.2 basis points and even though home prices and neighborhoods were unequal which contributed to unequal return on investment and wealth creation opportunities. In an era marked by systemic racism in housing and Jim Crow laws, the growth in Black homeownership was historically the greatest. The increase further resulted in the growth of homeownership rates for other communities across America. At the time, the events happening in the country enabled this boom, and as such, it is important we look back and filter out what can work in modern-day society.

- First, the economy was healthy, doing better in most areas.
- Secondly, the post-WWII housing boom was a contributing factor.
- Third, the government lifted a construction moratorium.
- Fourth, the government started issuing low-interest mortgage rates.

But, it is still important to highlight that even though there was an increase in Black homeownership, there was still some work to be done especially in bridging the gap between the Blacks and the whites. In 1940, the homeownership gap between African Americans and non-Hispanic whites was 22.6 percent. Two decades later, the gap had grown to 26 percent. After 1960, the African American rate of growth in homeownership began to stagnate. The Fair Housing Act of 1968 meant nothing. From 1960 to 1980, the African American homeownership rate only grew by six percentage points, from 38 percent to 43.8 percent.

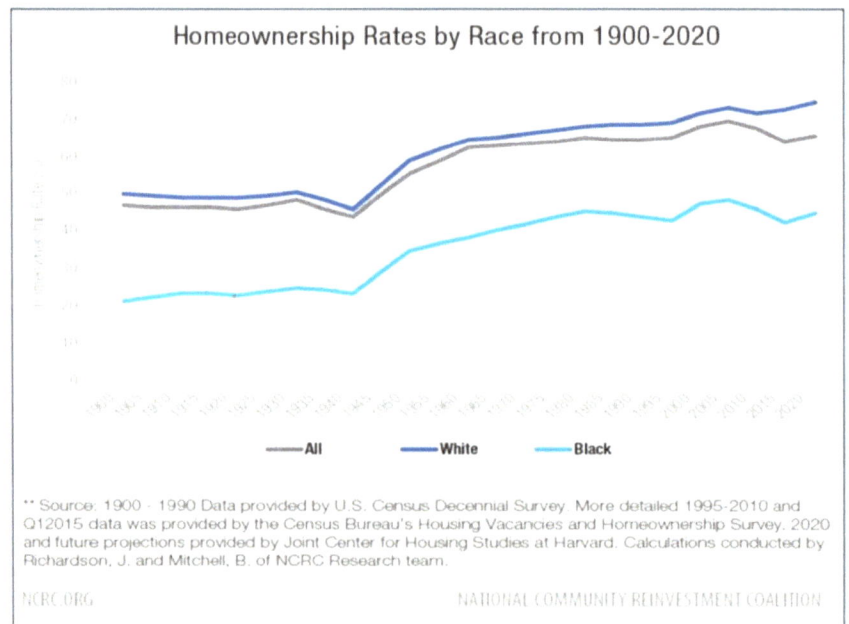

Homeownership Rates by Race from 1900-2020

All — White — Black

** Source: 1900 - 1990 Data provided by U.S. Census Decennial Survey. More detailed 1995-2010 and Q12015 data was provided by the Census Bureau's Housing Vacancies and Homeownership Survey. 2020 and future projections provided by Joint Center for Housing Studies at Harvard. Calculations conducted by Richardson, J. and Mitchell, B. of NCRC Research team.

NCRC.ORG   NATIONAL COMMUNITY REINVESTMENT COALITION

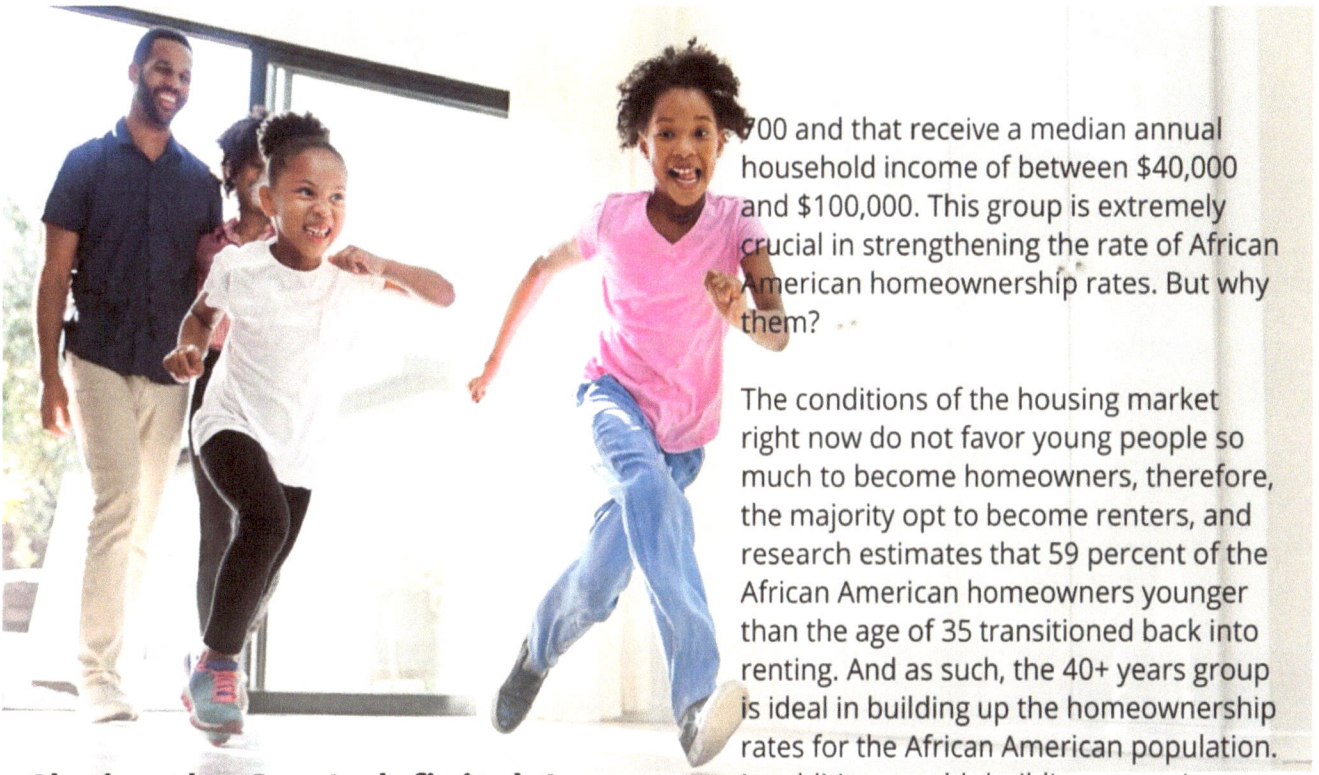

Closing the Gap Indefinitely!

The United States has to do better! It has to be that plain and simple, the government must make a deliberate effort to reverse the decline of the Black homeownership rates in the country, a trend that has been set and progressively supported over the last 20 years. Right now, amidst the COVID-19 pandemic, the people taking the hardest hits are the African Americans and Hispanics, and as such, the government must ensure that there is adequate home loss protection for its vulnerable communities, and it is especially critical—now more than ever. If such protection measures are enacted and carefully followed, the government will have not only ensured the economic stability of these families but also, it will have carved out a path of wealth protection for the low- to middle-income families. The 21st century saw a rise, a decline, and now what appears to be a stagnation in the African American homeownership rates, which means, there needs to be a renewed focus on advancing Black homeownership. This ultimately is the key to achieve a more equitable economy. One particular group that needs to be targeted is the African American households over the age of 40 with credit scores of between 600 and

700 and that receive a median annual household income of between $40,000 and $100,000. This group is extremely crucial in strengthening the rate of African American homeownership rates. But why them?

The conditions of the housing market right now do not favor young people so much to become homeowners, therefore, the majority opt to become renters, and research estimates that 59 percent of the African American homeowners younger than the age of 35 transitioned back into renting. And as such, the 40+ years group is ideal in building up the homeownership rates for the African American population. In addition, wealth-building campaigns focused on this group through homeownership could significantly improve their economic stability. Also, it is to be noted that most African American households are preferring the south and midwestern states. Thus, homeownership efforts should be focused on such areas. States like Michigan, Georgia, and Minnesota have the largest population of African American households.

Assuming we target that by the year 2040 we should have a 60 percent increase in the Black homeownership rate, this means that by the year 2030, there will be an additional three million new African American homeowners. However, this estimate by Urban Institute takes the 2019 data survey from the American Community Survey and assumes:

- That the Black population growth remains constant.
- That the average rate of African

American homeownership remains the same.

- That the household formation rate remains the same.
- And lastly, the homeownership loss rate for the African American community remains the same.

Currently, going to the data from ACS, there are about 41.98 million African Americans in the country, of which 6.4 million are homeowners. Urban Institute further goes to show that the additional 3 million new Black homeowners would create a total of almost 10 or 330,000 million a year. To reach this goal, it means that each year there needs to be an additional 165,000 new Black homeowners per year.

Achieving this target is not easy. It will require the concerted effort of everyone to invest in this campaign financially and promote programs and opportunities for the Black neighborhoods. Such programs include down payment assistance programs, and credit repair among many others. Such programs would go a long way to assist the African American people who are currently not able to afford or qualify for a home loan but can be mortgage-ready in the future. Today, The Power Is Now Media, Inc. promotes various HFAs in the state of California to bring awareness about the down payment assistance program and promises to expand the reach and include more outreach programs. The Power Is Now Media has entered into an agreement with the Golden State Finance Authority (GSFA) and California Housing Finance Agency (CalHFA) to leverage our media platform to educate minority communities about the various programs they can take advantage of at the state level in terms of down payment and closing cost assistance programs.

Additionally, there has been an increased focus on America's racial wealth divide and the gaps

in homeownership, and to be specific, many large banks have promised monetary incentives to create thousands of new Black homeowners. There needs to be a transformative investment and creative homeownership in areas where there is a concentration of African Americans with moderate incomes and lower credit scores but lack homeownership. These are the areas with the greatest room for improvement and represent a great possibility of African American growth in homeownership.

THE NATIONAL ASSOCIATION OF REAL ESTATE BROKERS
State of Housing in Black America Report

https://www.nareb.com/site-files/uploads/2020/10/2020-SHIBA-REPORT-OFFICIAL-COPY.pdf

Summary

- To put the Black-white homeownership gap further into perspective, in 2020 the gap was at an all-time high at 26 percentage points, less than one percent difference between the 26.8 percentage point gap in 1960, prior to the passage of the 1968 Fair Housing Act.
- The majority of Black Americans are concentrated in 20 Metropolitan Statistical Areas (MSAs). The Dallas-Fort Worth and Arlington area make the list.
- Considerable evidence has shown that

overall homes tend to have lower value in predominantly Black neighborhoods than in neighborhoods with lower minority concentrations.

- What's more, as more minority residents move into the neighborhood, housing appreciation also tends to decline.
- Despite lower homeownership rates than previous generations, 89 percent of Black millennials report their intentions of becoming homeowners eventually.

Introduction

Homeownership allows families to accumulate money, aids community stabilization, connects homeowners to greater educational and career prospects and physical and mental wellness. The housing market and its financing are important components of a healthy economy; it also employs thousands of people and generates income for industry experts and profits for investors. Despite popular culture, and politicians' focus on this part of the "American Dream," Black and other minority families have experienced several impediments to homeownership, most of which may be related to cumulative poverty and systemic inequality. Homeownership options for Black Americans have started to improve in the years after the 2008 financial crisis. However, the COVID-19 pandemic started to endanger the lives, health, and economic viability of Black families throughout the United States in early 2020.

Current State of Ownership:

Homeownership and credit access disparities contribute to overall wealth disparity. Black homeownership peaked at 47% in 2020 but has yet to return to pre-crisis levels.

In 2019, the homeownership rate for Black, Latinx, and white families was 42.1 percent for Black, 47.5 percent for Latinx, and 73.4 percent for white families—according to the U.S. Census Bureau. According to Census projections for the second quarter of 2020, Black homeowners account for 47.0 percent of all households, while non-Hispanic white households account for 76.0 percent. In 2020, the Black-white homeownership disparity was 26 percent, somewhat lower than the 26.8 percentage point divide in 1960, before implementing the 1968 Fair Housing Act. In owner homes, Blacks are underrepresented. New Black homebuyers account for fewer than half of all Black families in the United States (13 percent).

Age:

Homeownership rates among younger Black families are particularly low. The homeownership disparity between Black and white people is wide across all age categories. The lowest disparity exists among people over 65, indicating that Blacks become homeowners later in life. Nonetheless, 62.4 percent of Blacks over 65 own their homes, compared to 81.4 percent of whites in this age bracket. Black householders under the age of 35 have lower homeownership rates than other demographics.

Gender:

Blacks have a larger percentage of female-headed owner families than any other group of owner families. In comparison to other racial and ethnic groupings, however, the gender disparity in homeownership is minimal.

Education:

Black college graduates have a homeownership rate of just 3.2 percentage points greater than white high school dropouts. 86.4 percent of Black college students owe money on student loans. Only 14 percent of African American graduates could escape student debts in 2015–2016, even though 29% of bachelor's degree holders were debt-free. Compared to 18 percent of white graduates and 13 percent of Hispanic graduates, 33% of African American bachelor's degree holders owe $40,000 or more in debt.

Earnings and Wealth:

The homeownership gap is said to be primarily caused by racial disparities in income and wealth. The cumulative impacts of these glaring discrepancies are shown in mortgage credit availability and homeownership possibilities. In 2018, Black households had a median income that was 40% lower than white households' median income, while white households had a median net worth ten times larger than Black households' median net worth. According to the Federal Reserve, nearly 20% of Black families have no or negative net worth, compared to just 9% of white families.

Geographic Location:

In the United States, the Black population is concentrated in big cities. Los Angeles has a homeownership rate of 31.9 percent, whereas Richmond, Virginia, has 49.8 percent. It's also worth mentioning that 25.6 percent of the Black population lived in locations with median home prices higher than the national average of $253,000 in 2019. Many of these metro regions are significantly racially stratified. Greater homeownership differences are sometimes associated with larger levels of segregation, as shown in New York, Chicago, Detroit, St. Louis,

and Cleveland. Black homeowners have lower median and mean house values than other racial/ethnic groupings. Black homebuyers are less likely to qualify for bigger mortgage loans or more costly houses due to lower salaries, wealth levels, and other credit limits. According to past studies, home values in largely Black communities tend to be lower than values in similarly located communities with smaller minority populations.

Opportunities in the Market:

Black homebuyers received around 472,000 house purchase mortgages in 2019, totaling over $113 billion in house acquisitions. These estimates reflect a possible real estate investment of $6.8 billion.

National Association of Real Estate Brokers:

Real estate professionals who service these neighborhoods may benefit from ES-3 commissions and other possibilities. Between 2018 and 2019, the number of loan applications and originations for Black homebuyers almost doubled; further, the number of loan applications and originations for Black borrowers in the South was almost double that of the West, Northeast, and Midwest combined. Despite having lower homeownership rates than prior generations and postponing house purchases by seven years or more, 89 percent of millennials say they want to become homeowners at some point. The Atlanta, DC, Dallas, and Miami metropolitan regions have the greatest concentrations of this demographic group.

Around 17% of Black families in the United States had an annual income of more than $110,000. These households are concentrated in a limited number of metropolitan locations, such as the Washington, DC and Atlanta regions. According to Freddie Mac, there were over 2.9 million Black mortgage-ready families in the United States in 2019. Potential homebuyers under 45 years old who live in a geographically affordable location with an appropriate supply of homes and have the necessary income and credit history are eligible.

State of the Black Borrower Mortgage Market:

The essential aspects of the mortgage market for Black borrowers are highlighted in this section.

Rates of Interest:

According to HMDA statistics from 2018, Black borrowers pay considerably higher FHA loans and somewhat higher rates for conventional loans. Disparities based on borrower race are more important than those based just on ethnicity. For example, Black non-Hispanic borrowers paid an average of 5.52 percent in FHA loans, whereas Black Latinx borrowers paid an average of 4.87 percent. White Latinx borrowers paid an average of $4.91 for an FHA loan compared to $4.83 for white non-Latinx borrowers. Black non-Latinx borrowers and white Latinx borrowers paid higher interest rates on conventional loans than white non-Latinx borrowers.

Denials of Mortgage Loans:

Black candidates are more than twice as likely to be rejected as white candidates, which has been the case for a long time. DTI and credit history are the most prevalent causes for loan denial, regardless of race or ethnicity. In contrast, the percent of rejections due to DTI and credit history are much greater for Black applicants. In addition, Black candidates were less likely than white candidates to be turned down owing to collateral difficulties or incomplete applications.

Income:

In 2018, Black Hispanic/Latinx FHA borrowers earned an average of $149,000 per year, while Black non-Hispanic FHA borrowers earned $103,000 per year. The average income of white non-Hispanic FHA borrowers was $140,000, while the average income of white Hispanic FHA borrowers was $167,000. In addition, Black borrowers in the conventional market earn $65,000 a year more than Black borrowers in the FHA market. The earnings of Black homebuyers and owners are lower than those of white homebuyers and owners.

Loan Amount:

For Black and Black Hispanic borrowers, the average single-family home purchase loan amount in 2018 was $206,000 for FHA and $214,000 and $208,000 for conventional originations, respectively. White FHA homeowners took up $190,000 in FHA loans and $270,000 in conventional loans on average.

LTV Ratios and Down Payments:

On average, Black homebuyers have higher LTVs, which corresponds to a greater share of FHA loans. The typical down payment for Black homebuyers is 3.5 percent, reflecting that the FHA or VA insures nearly 53% of mortgages issued to Black borrowers.

White purchasers, on the other hand, made a 10% down payment on their homes in 2018. Loans to Black borrowers are far more likely to have LTVs of more than 90%.

Conclusion

Racial disparities in income and wealth primarily cause the homeownership gap.

Through income and down payment and reserve requirements, debt-to-income (DTI) ratios, loan-to-value (LTV) ratios, and credit history, the cumulative impact of these severe discrepancies reveal themselves in access to mortgage financing and homeownership chances. Black household income and net worth are much lower than white family income and net worth. In 2018, for example, Black families had a median income that was 40% lower than that of white families. The impacts of cumulative disadvantage may be seen in wealth differences as well. In 2018, white households had a median net worth ten times greater than Black households' median net worth. According to the Federal Reserve, nearly 20% of Black families have no or negative net worth, compared to just 9% of white families.

Where We Will Start:

The Power Is Now Media Inc. is based in Riverside, California so we will start there. California's Black homeownership rate today is lower now than it was in the 1960s when it was completely legal to discriminate against Black homebuyers.

California's history of housing discrimination against African Americans is one significant reason that the rate of homeownership is lowest among all minority groups. African Americans were specifically targeted and denied access to housing because of exclusionary housing policies and practices beginning with the first Governor of California, Peter Hardeman Burnett, who supported the abolishment of slavery but openly stated and ran on a platform that he did not want African Americans in California. California adopted every tactic in the book for Government-sponsored redlining, racist covenants restricting the sale of the property to whites only, and predatory lending. African Americans'

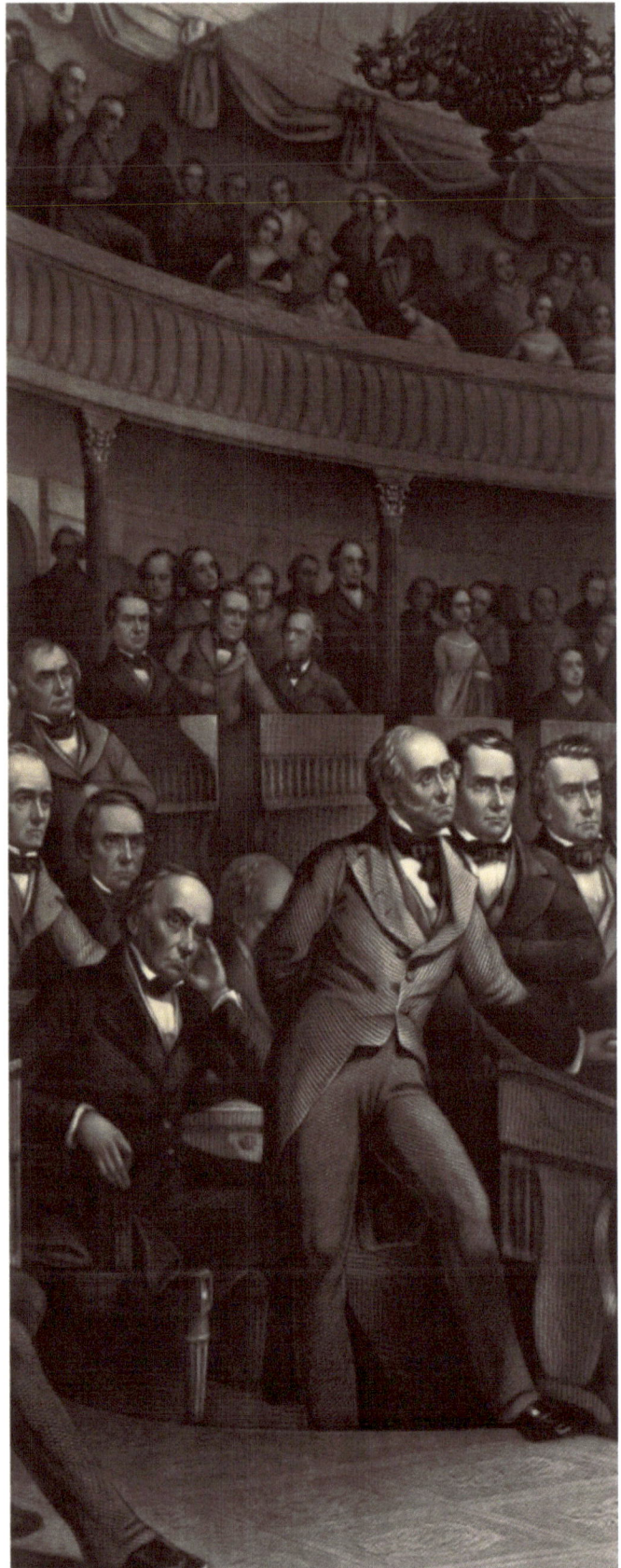

homeownership rate in California today is a reflection of discrimination that has resulted in the lost opportunity to build generational wealth.

It would take legal action and legislation to confront the problems of racism in California. In order for us to understand the effects of racism (systemic and institutional), we have to understand the long history of racism in California, though once hailed as a free state.

Our beautiful state of California has always been adored and hailed as a landscape of liberty and a place where people could escape to—to enjoy the economic and social benefits. California has always been the epitome of unlimited opportunities for financial freedom and upward growth for the people that finally make it to the state. Indeed, even for the 'slaves' in other areas, California seemed like the beacon of hope and a place where they could call home, in fact, for Sandy Jones, Robert, and Carter Perkins, the gold rush seemed to present the opportunities for the future. The three were former slaves from Mississippi. In 1851, they arrived in the small town of Ophir, California, and set up their operations there. The three would later build a booming freight business transporting supplies across Northern California and within just a few months, each had managed to amass a personal fortune of over $3,000 in personal property, including a mule team and a wagon. Not so long afterward, the three African American men's dreams and aspirations came to a sudden end in a late-night raid in April 1852. In their sleep, a group of armed white men broke into their cabin, tied them up and loaded them into their own wagon, and took them to Sacramento using their own mule team. The judge in Sacramento pronounced them as fugitive slaves and ordered their deportation back to the Slave South!

Just six weeks earlier, the state had passed a new Fugitive Slave Law that decreed that any enslaved Black people who had entered California when it was still a territory had no legal right to freedom even though the state was a free state.

History records that California came into the union in 1850 as a "free state" and slavery were the evil happening in the southern states or so we thought. Yet, famed for its liberal position, California has a far darker history than we can admit. A year earlier, Peter Burnett took the podium in Sacramento in 1849 and faced the pioneering team which was determined to take the state from an upstart territory to a fully-fledged state. A day before, Peter had been elected California's first governor and while addressing the legislators, he sparked one of California's most controversial issues of his time—the place of African Americans in the future state. Burnett, a former slaveholder from Tennessee, had a burning passion to create a white-only American West.

A White Supremacist in Office

Burnett was elected a legislature in Oregon and took an active lead in passing a law that prohibited African Americans from the state. This law allowed the slaveholders to keep slaves for just three years after which the slaves would be liberated and required to leave the state. If African Americans refused to leave the state, they would be tortured, and this is how the law earned its "Peter Hardeman Burnett's Lash Law." Even though this law was rescinded, it was followed by other Black exclusionary laws. Five years later, Burnett joined the gold tailspin to California where he befriended John Sutter Jr. and helped him found Sacramento. He was then elected the Governor of California and in his new position, he once again tried to pass the laws banning African Americans but was unsuccessful. He was also a catalyst for the genocide of California's indigenous population. Burnett signed the perversely named Act for the Government and Protection of Indians. The law allowed white people to force the natives from their lands into indentured servitude. Under his leadership, the U.S. Cavalry troops slaughtered native Californians including the Pomo tribe members in the "Bloody Island Massacre." Burnett would later end up in California's Supreme Court and was in fact on the sitting bench that ordered the infamous deportation of fugitive slave Archy Lee—in violation of California's constitution. And while his actions were extreme and a vision of exclusively white west, it was fitting the broader white supremacist policies of the time.

A "Free" State . . . Not So Free

After All!

California decided to ban slavery after a very heated debate. But in his vision, Burnett did not include African Americans at all. "It could be no favor, and no kindness, to permit [free Blacks] to settle in the state," he said, "while it would be a most serious injury to us . . . Had they been born here, and had acquired rights, in consequence, I should not recommend any measures to expel them . . . the object is to keep them out." But, as previously mentioned, Burnett wasn't alone in his idea of a white-only west, throughout the 1840s and 1850s, California citizens and legislators fought to ensure that African Americans were banned from entering or even living in California. And while most of them failed, the fear and

racism inflicted on the Black population were unfathomed.

The state was a free state, and by all means, it held both opportunities and real dangers for the people of color. Note: many of the Black people in the state at the time were free former slaves. The move to ban African Americans from the state was a culmination of the state's conflict over whether to allow slavery as an institution or not. At the same time, there was a national debate raging over how to decide if the United States' newest territories should be open to slavery, and the opinion was split into two; the pro-slavery advocates—mostly from the southern states and the "free soilers"—abolitionists who were very determined to introduce slave-free states into the union. The debate became heated as it encroached on the western states. In 1849, California threatened the balance between the free states and the slave states. California entered the union as part of the Compromise of 1850, to keep the interests of the slave owners and the abolitionists in balance. Still, that wasn't the break African Americans were hoping for because it did not end the virulent racism they faced in the state. As the state drew its constitution, it again faced these issues and here, many of the legislature who were once inclined to the idea of a world with no slavery, and where all men were equal, called for the new state to bar African Americans from the state altogether. This ultimately resulted in the segregation of African Americans, especially the miners, as some were worried that Black miners would pool their resources together and wield more influence than the white miners. Thus, they were driven out of town and subjected to segregation. A growing minority wanted African Americans to be banned from the new state.

Historian Eugene H. Berwanger records that

the very question of whether to allow African Americans who were free to live in the state was only an issue that sparked a contentious debate at California's Constitutional Convention. At the time, Morton M. McCarver—a Kentuckian—brought a resolution to the table and suggested that Blacks should be excluded from the state. It should be noted that McCarver was inspired by Oregon's law barring African Americans from the state. "Depending on it, you will find the country flooded with a population of free Negroes," said McCarver, calling that potential wave of immigration "the greatest calamity that could befall California."

Staying in California was an issue of life and death for the African Americans, and even after the passage of the California Constitution that forbade slavery, there was still some gray line in the question of rights for the African Americans that caused a deep divide in the state. And sometimes, that divide would boil over into personal rivalries. For instance, in 1859, an argument over slavery caused a duel when senator David C. Broderick, an abolitionist was killed by ex-chief Justice of the state of California David S. Terry, a pro-slavery advocate. Throughout his tenure as California Governor, Burnett tried over and over again to exclude Blacks from the state. It did not stop with him, his successor also tried and failed. In addition, Isaac Allen even brought forward a bill that alleged that an association with the white people would lead to fostering the ignorance and pride of the free African Americans "so that he becomes insolent and defiant, and if insufficient numbers, would become dangerous."

For now, the African American community in California was 'safe,' however, the issue of whether slavery should be introduced in the state remained incendiary.

Housing Discrimination in California

Even though the civil rights movement ended institutionalized racism in America in 1964, a century after the abolishment of slavery, racial discrimination was still happening openly in many neighborhoods. The law passed then protected the constitutional rights of all Americans and enforced provisions preventing the discrimination of people at the federal level but that wasn't extended to the housing markets. California however was progressive, passing the California Fair Housing Act of 1963 also known as the Rumford Act (AB1240) because of its sponsor, assemblyman William Bryon Rumford. The bill was one of the most significant and sweeping that saw the rights of the African American and other people of color protected wherein they could purchase a home without discrimination of any sort.

The California Fair Housing Act of 1963 was enacted largely in response to 'failure' or

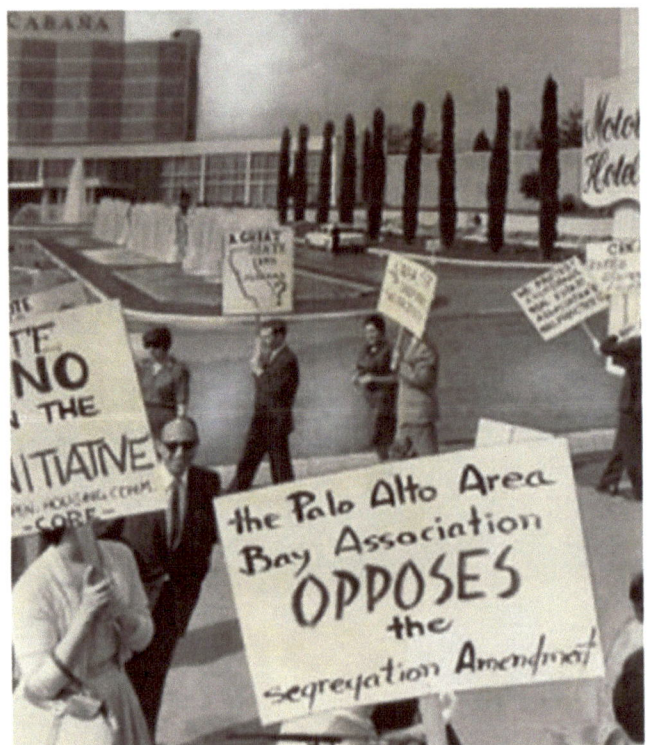

earlier fair housing legislation and evolved from a larger civil rights struggle that emerged over the movement to create a permanent Fair Employment Practices Commission (FEPC) at the state level between 1946 and 1959. In the state of California, several activists called for much stronger and fair housing laws than the measures that were put forward in 1959 and 1960. This campaign paralleled others happening concurrently in Washington, Michigan, and Ohio. The Rumford Act was a call to stop discrimination in all public and private housing in the state and was immediately met with opposition in the state's legislature. Most Republicans exempted most forms of private and single-family housing before the bill was passed in September 1963. This new law prohibited discrimination in the public housing sector and also in all residential properties with more than 5 units.

The California Real Estate Association (CREA) would then launch a repeal campaign. By exploiting the growing hostility towards all the liberal social programs and promoting the call for 'property owner rights' the CREA-led effort resulted in the creation of the Proposition 14 referendum towards the end of 1964 and the Rumford Act was repealed. Two years later, the Rumford Act was restored when the California Supreme Court ruled Proposition 14 as illegal. A year later, the decision by the supreme court was bolstered stating that Proposition 14 violated the 14th Amendment and the Civil Rights Act of 1866 which "prohibits all racial discrimination in the sale or rental of property."

It would also require that leaders in the private sector, large corporations, for-profit and nonprofit organizations, and the state government change their policies and take the initiative to make life better for African Americans and to make homeownership a reality. In recognition and support of the 1968 National Fair Housing Act, the 1963 California Rumford Fair Housing Act, and the 1959 California Unruh Civil Rights Act, and the many people who have fought for civil rights and the basic rights and freedom for every Black Californian to own a home, The Power Is Now is launching our Power Is Now African American Wealth Initiative and campaign for Black homeownership in California.

The purpose of the campaign is to address the significant gap between African Americans and other ethnic groups and to provide information, education, and support to make a difference and close the gap. The greatest barrier to homeownership is the down payment. The second barrier would be financial literacy and education about down payment assistance and HUD counseling opportunities to address credit and money management. These issues transcend race and ethnicity but have had a disparate impact on African Americans because of systematic racism at the highest level of government and the private sector; especially regarding housing.

Five Key Objectives of the African American Wealth Initiative

1. Knowledge

Knowledge is the Power you need to build wealth. Knowledge always comes before money if you want to retain the wealth you establish.

2. Commitment to Financial Independence

We must take Individual responsibility for our lives. Commitment requires discipline, and discipline requires a budget and accountability.

3. Investment in real estate

We must prioritize ownership in real property as opposed to personal property. Real property appreciates, and personal property depreciates.

4. Financial and Credit Management

We must live within our means and not abuse credit. Credit is not income - It is a convenience for cash. Good credit is the beginning of building wealth. Good credit is a FICO Score of 720 to 799 higher. Great credit is 800 to 850.

5. Creating Wealth

We must understand that wealth is a mindset that becomes an asset and becomes a legacy over time. Buy and Hold, or Buy, Sell to Buy again and hold - making not spending – creating a legacy of wealth and not leaving poverty. We must be intentional about leaving a legacy of wealth and an inheritance for our family. It will not happen by accident but by planning, investing, and learning over time.

The Power to Start and the Power To Stop

To achieve these objectives, we help change our community's mindset and help them believe that The Power to Buy is Now but will require a change in behaviors.

The Power to Start

Knowledge.

Knowledge is the necessary foundation to homeownership. With it, minorities could take control of their families' future for generations to come.

Start believing that homeownership is achievable.

Some may see it as an extreme sport to buy a house in 2021 because of low inventory, but the truth is, it's not impossible. The demand for houses has gone up as people take advantage of the low mortgage rates and the desire brought on by the pandemic to settle down in rural areas and larger spaces because they can now work from home.

With the low housing inventory and the insatiable demand for homes, there will be a lot of bidding wars on the listed houses. Navigating the market successfully, as it is, will require you to be flexible with what you want and for you to make concessions to get what you need. Also, make offers on homes you are sure that you can afford. Many programs are available for downpayment assistance and affordable mortgages that everyone can access when pointed in the right direction.

Start acting instead of procrastinating.

House prices have been on the rise since the beginning of the pandemic. It's understandable to want to wait for the prices to fall before leaping. It is, however, not guaranteed that they will fall. If anything, the prices are set to soar even further. April 2021 saw the home prices rise 8.2% from the same time last year.

Moreover, mortgage rates are more likely to remain low, averaging 3%, making it an ideal time to buy a home. Also, you can take advantage of reducing your taxes and building wealth by being on the receiving end of the payments you are making in rent.

Commitment to finncil independence.

Commitment to making a change for yourself and future generations is a must. Anything worth doing takes work, but you can find yourself among other homeowners with a bit of effort and leave the renting life behind for good.

Start living within your means & not for others.

If your dream of owning a house in America is going to become a reality, then you need to live a lifestyle you can sustain easily. This means spending less than you earn and not the other way round or, in other words, living within your means.

This will require you to restructure your life to be more conscious of how you choose to spend your money. To be effective, you need to know how much money you

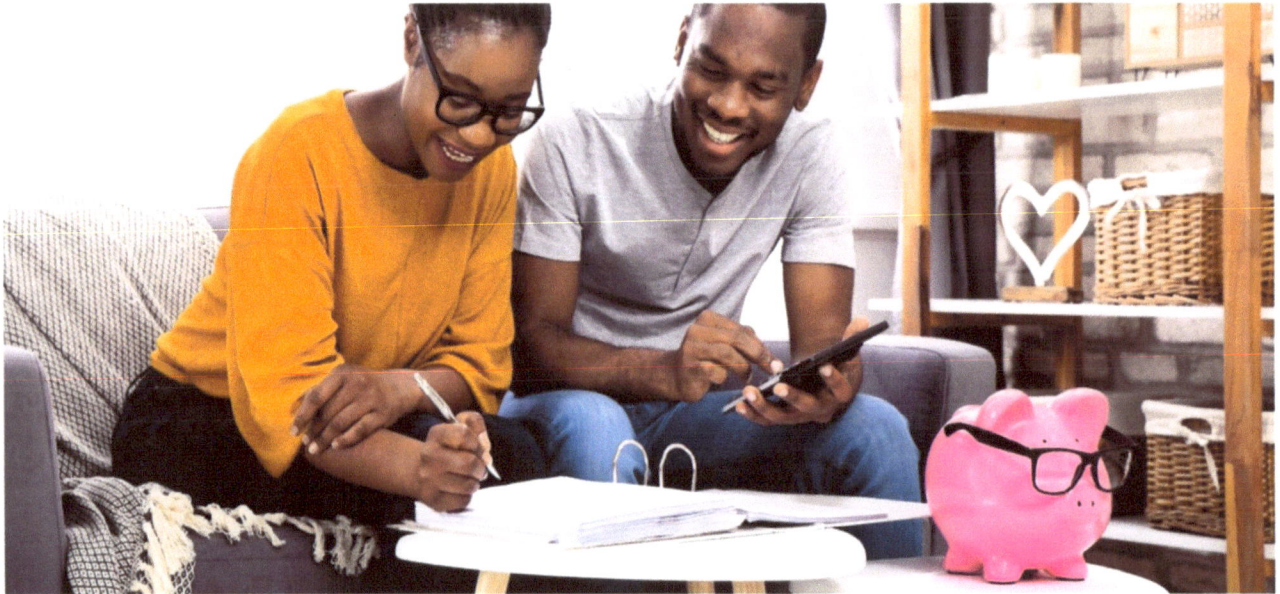

make, the money you actually spend, and stop relying on credit cards. Establish a budget that will ensure that you can pay your expenses and save money. It will not be easy, but it is absolutely necessary.

Financial and credit management is necessary for everyone who wants to own a home. The good news is that financial and credit management are learned skills everyone can acquire.

Start living on a budget and create a plan.

Having a great budget is instrumental in achieving your dream of owning a new home. It is indeed a step in the right direction in managing your finances towards your goal, especially if you're saving for the American dream of homeownership. It does, however, require you to have a written budget. I recommend www.mint.com as a great way to go beyond typing on spreadsheets or writing things down on paper. Creating an online budget gives you instant access to data, so you know where you are at all times.

The first step is to download the program. It is free. It will enable you to carefully assess your income, expenses, and debts once you complete the setup. Now you can make sound decisions of what adjustments and changes will need to be made to reach your savings and down payment targets. Once the plan is set, you must agree to meet frequently with your spouse and family to discuss the state of the family's financial status. A plan without action and accountability will end up in the pile of other dreams that have never been realized.

Start saving money for emergencies.

Unexpected financial expenses are guaranteed to happen and can be a nightmare if you do not have an emergency fund to break the fall. You may buy a home and find that it requires repairs you didn't know about. If you spend all the money you had on the down payment and closing

costs, then it will result in a cascade of other financial problems. It is therefore prudent to set money aside before buying a home that covers financial emergencies too.

This is not easy if you have been living an undisciplined life. Financial discipline is required to save money and build an emergency fund. One strategy to save money is to set up an automated savings account in your bank so that you do not have to think about putting money away.

Start paying off your credit card debt.

Most Americans are in debt in one way or another. It is, however, worth noting that lenders pay close attention to the debt-to-income ratio (DTI) of borrowers applying for a mortgage loan. The higher the ratio, the more likely your application will be denied. This is because a high amount of debt makes the lender conclude that you will have difficulty making the monthly mortgage installment. Therefore, if you are going to make a mortgage application, it is necessary to pay off your credit card debt as early as possible.

Clear the balance every month and eventually stop using them altogether. Credit is a convenience for cash. With the advent of Visa Debit Cards, it is no longer convenient for cash because you can just use your debit card. So stop using them entirely because they can add to your debt-to-income ratio (DTI). Your housing expense ratio, the total house payment divided into your gross income, should be no higher than 35% to 40% of your gross income.

Your total debt to income ratio, including credit cards, student loans, auto loans, and personal loans, should not be greater than 40 to 45%. Other debt like child support, alimony, and delinquent taxes are also added to the total debt ratio. Not only will having a low DTI on both ends make your loan application more attractive, but it will enable you to qualify for many down payment and closing costs assistance programs.

Start working on restoring & maintain your credit score.

A high credit score is essential in the home buying journey. Therefore, you should aim to have a great credit score by paying your bills on time, avoiding defaulting on loans, and not carrying any credit card balances. This will ensure that you have the highest FICO® Score. This dramatically influences your attractiveness to lenders. Typically, a credit score ranges between 300-850. It is therefore advisable to have one closer to 850. This will give your lender the confidence that you will be able to service the loan.

You can use lender credit to finance your closing costs. You essentially agree to pay a higher rate than you can afford to get a credit back interest that you can use for closing costs. When you have a high credit score, this can be a great benefit and reduce your cash to close on a purchase or refinance transaction. The best benefit of having a high credit score is that your bank can offer you a loan with a low-interest rate.

Creating wealth

Creating wealth is not going to happen overnight. It will only happen when you intentionally decide to make lasting changes about money and wealth.

Start reading and studying about money & wealth.

Saving involves a lot more than putting aside money. It also requires you to know where your money is going (budget), how to save it (automatic deposits) and where to invest it. It is important that you become financially literate to avoid making catastrophic investment decisions that could have long-term consequences. It doesn't always have to be about what to avoid but what to do.

Therefore, by amassing knowledge, one can plan their finances, manage their debt, and make investment decisions. Becoming financially literate is not just taking a college course or online classes. It is a lifelong commitment because the economy is constantly changing and bringing new challenges and opportunities. Only knowledge and networking with others with knowledge and who have the same goals can help you achieve your goals.

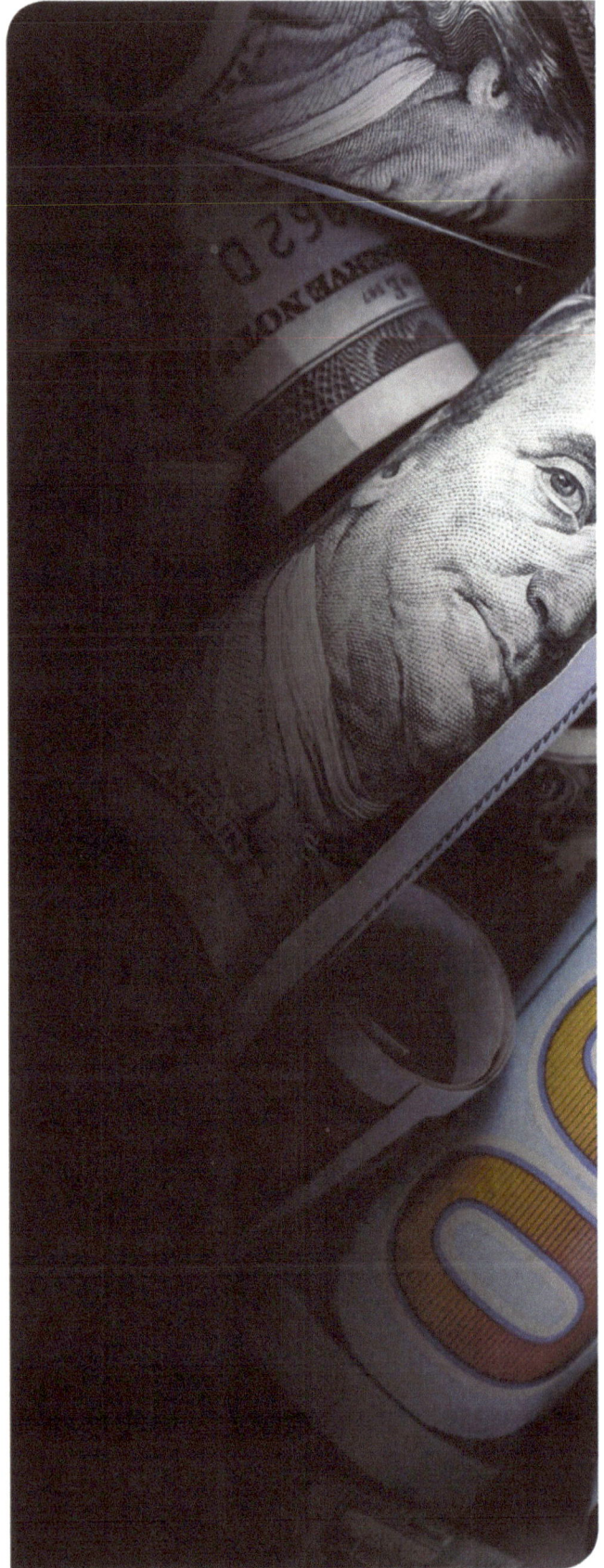

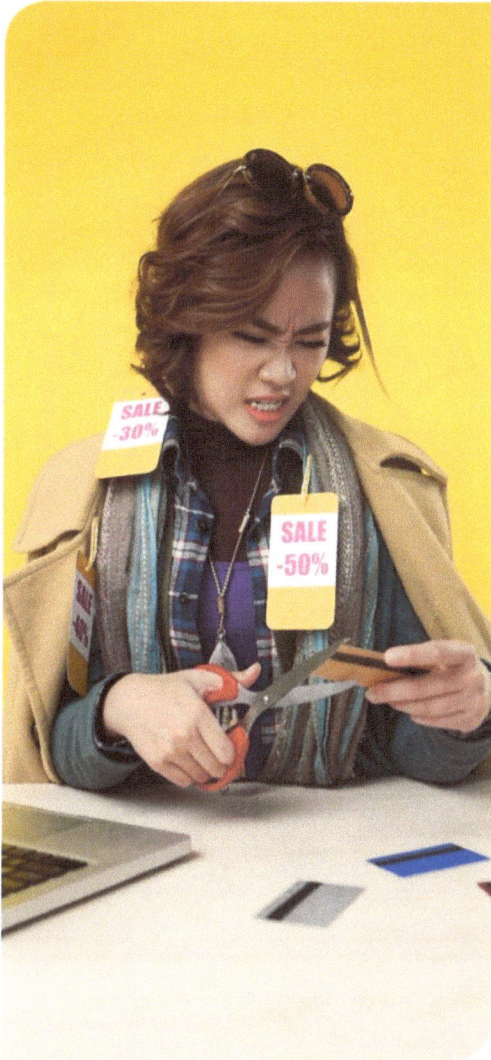

This will give you a better picture of where your money is going. Once that is clear, you will need to make a priority list of all the essential expenses. In other words, stop spending money where there's no necessity.

Stop going out to eat every day for lunch.

It is always going to be easier to eat out instead of making a nice homemade meal for lunch or dinner. It may be easy, yes, but it is the most expensive option of the two. Imagine eating food worth above $20 every single day. That means, in five days, you'll have spent more than $100 on food alone. You may not realize it, but that is a lot of money you could have used elsewhere.

It is not going to be an easy fit to quit this highly addictive behavior, but it is essential. You will want to stay clear of social pressures that might trigger you; you are going to have to learn a few simple recipes, and a nice meal plan should help you figure out what you are going to make. It sounds like a lot of work, but the money you save makes it worth it.

Stop financing clothes and shoes pay cash.

We all like to look good. But at what cost? Fashion trends often push us to impulse purchases of clothes and shoes that we do not need. Ultimately, it leaves you with a closet full of clothes and in a ton of debt or unnecessary expenditure.

So, instead of using the debit card or credit card to make these purchases, why don't you save up for that pair of shoes or outfit. It will give you time to reflect on whether the purchase was worth it. Also beneficial is taking care of the clothes and shoes you already have. It eliminates the chance of you needing to replace them.

The Power To Stop

Stop spending money indiscriminately.

No doubt, this is going to be difficult. In a world where you are surrounded by a spending culture and persuasive advertisements of products you need to buy, you are bound to be tempted. But for the sake of a healthy financial future, you will need to adjust your spending habits. Something that you could find helpful is creating a list of expenses with their respective receipts in hand.

Stop financing cars, and vacations pay cash.

So, you want a car but can you afford it? Financing may be the easier option, but it could leave you with a hole of debt. Did you know that 85% of cars purchased are financed? Meaning approximately every hour, an American is working to earn money needed for the car loan of the car that took them to work in the first place. Imagine being in debt because of something that depreciates in value. Paying cash is the better option.

The same applies to vacation. Write down the costs you need for that getaway. Save for a couple of months and enjoy a perfect holiday debt-free.

Stop all auto pays from your checking account.

At least 61% of Americans have at least one bill in auto payment. It is convenient and a great way to maintain a good credit score. As much as they are good, they can be a costly mistake. If a company billed $850 instead of the usual $85, would you notice? Imagine also paying for a service you no longer use.

Therefore, to stay in control of your finances, you may have to stop auto pays, which is not hard to do. Write and call the company to notify them that you have withdrawn permission for them to take payment, write and call your bank, give the bank a 'stop payment order' and monitor your account.

Stop paying cable & monthly Memberships.

We all love good entertainment, but cable is expensive. You will likely save $1200 in a month if you made a $100 monthly payment by cutting out cable. That money would be better placed in your savings account for a house down payment. If you can't go cold turkey, you could substitute cable with streaming services that only need a strong internet connection.

To make more savings, you will have to carefully monitor your account for memberships that you don't need anymore and cancel them. For example, if you pay a gym membership and haven't been there for over a year, it is time to cancel.

Stop making excuses for where you are.

Making excuses is a common human response when there is the fear of the unknown or when one falls short of meeting a goal. And definitely, that's not a good habit. Let's face it! It's time to take accountability for your actions and make peace with them. This may require you to identify why you haven't been able to get your new house and make changes.

If you have a terrible spending habit, you are going to take accountability and make the necessary changes.If you are afraid of leaping to buy a new home, reading on it should clarify the technicalities involved. This will make you very confident in working towards your goal.

Stop complaining and get help.

Complaining is counterintuitive to your success. It gives you a sense of hopelessness that makes it difficult to chase your dreams. If you are hoping to buy a house, you need to stop complaining. The market may be terrible, but by complaining, you change nothing.

The process of homeownership can be complicated, and it is perfectly okay to ask for help. Asking for help doesn't mean you lose control; it just means someone guides you through the process. It could be your realtor or the financial lender of your choice. If it has something to do with how you spend money, have a third party such as a financial advisor look over your finances and tell you where to make cuts or spend accordingly.

Stop hoping for solutions because hope is not a strategy.

Hope is good, but it is not a strategy. What you need to have is an actionable plan that brings your American dream of ownership closer to becoming a reality. You should make sure that your plan is evident on the how and when you hope to accomplish your dream. It also needs to be adaptable to changes in market trends. It also should include how much you intend to save and for how long. It also offers a great roadmap to your destination.

Furthermore, when you feel overwhelmed, it provides a nice base to check on the progress you have made.

10 Point Wealth Building Pledge

I, **(state your name)**, from this day forward, declare before my God, my family, and my community a renewed commitment to build wealth and to leave a legacy and an inheritance for my family and my community.

I pledge the following:

1. To save and invest 10 to 20 percent of my after-tax income.
2. To be a proactive and informed investor in real estate.
3. To be a disciplined and knowledgeable consumer in my spending.
4. To measure my personal wealth by net worth and not my income.
5. To engage in sound budgeting, credit, and tax management practices.
6. To teach business & financial principles to my children & demonstrate them in my actions.
7. To use a portion of my wealth to strengthen my family and community.
8. To be humble and not live extravagantly saving instead of consuming.
9. To ensure my wealth is passed onto my family and my community.
10. To maximize my earning power through a commitment to financial literacy and professional development.

Our Media Strategy to Improve Minority Homeownership

The Power Is Now Media is committed to supporting minority groups achieve the dream of homeownership, with a particular focus on the African American Community. Homeownership is a dream for many African Americans denied because of the long history of racism and discrimination in the United States.

Our strategy is to use our online platform to provide media support to organizations that desire to see the rate of homeownership increase for African Americans. We will promote, support, educate and inspire the African American community to achieve the dream of homeownership in partnership with community organizations that have established relationships and access to the African American community. Our platform will become a media extension to amplify the voices of Black civic & community leaders, business leaders, political leaders, religious leaders, Black Real Estate professionals, and all organizations who are advocates for homeownership.

How We Will Start

The African American Wealth Initiative will begin with a series of educational videos, podcasts, magazine articles, and virtual workshops for homebuyers. The series will explain the availability and requirements for homeownership financing, down payment assistance, financial education, and budgeting through HUD counseling.

Helping First-Time Homebuyers to obtain the money for a down payment and closing costs

The Power Is Now Media will ally with three key groups currently providing affordable housing programs and products or support services for potential homebuyers.

These are:

1. Housing finance agencies throughout the United States
2. Non Profit organizations that are acting as administrators of state and federal funded grants and programs; and
3. HUD-approved counseling agencies

The alliance aims to promote and advertise the accessibility of funds available for down payment assistance, closing cost assistance, First Time Homebuyer counseling, credit restoration services, and other services they currently provide.

How we will help First Time Homebuyers after the close of Escrow What we have done and are doing

To help First-Time Homebuyers, The Power Is Now Media has formed alliances with black real estate professionals across the country. These are experienced real estate professionals who desire to serve the communities in which they are from or currently live. In our platform, we give them the opportunity to speak via podcast and video about their market areas and the real estate opportunities that exist and about listing opportunities that they currently have to give first-time homebuyers and minorities an opportunity to buy.

The Power Is Now Media is currently working with churches in California and has put on virtual seminars and live seminars at the church facility to educate consumers about homeownership and credit and revive programmatic information.

The Power Is Now Media has established a pastoral alliance with ministers who have participated with us in the past. We are building on that alliance to increase our pastoral membership to over 500 pastors serving congregations throughout the United States. Our goal is to be an affiliate of every church to provide them the resources that will enable them to support ongoing training and education to their congregation to become homeowners.

The Power Is Now African American Wealth Initiative Resources

The Power Is Now Media will be creating homebuyer resources to support attendees of the seminars. Each attendee will receive the recorded video and podcast of all events and transcriptions of all events in the form of e-books—also, additional resources from our speakers and sponsors of the virtual and live homebuyer workshops.

Black, Minority, LBGTQ+ Agents Directory

We will form an online Directory of full-time professional agents with experience working with buyers and who join the African American Wealth Initiative.

The power of African American Wealth Initiative will kick off a national effort to create financial independence for African-Americans by supporting the value and importance of homeownership and increasing the rate of homeownership.

We will form alliances with major companies that provide support to new homeowners to help them reduce or possibly eliminate the cost associated with the furnishing, buying appliances, repairing, securing landscaping, and stocking the home with food, cleaning, and home supplies.

These costs can be high and impact the borrower's ability to save money and cause them to increase their debt and debt-to-income ratio to meet the regular everyday needs of the family.

These companies will include non-profit organizations that have set aside funding for low to moderate-income communities for these very purposes. It will also provide an opportunity for other organizations to create fun. Major retailers in the furniture space will be able to provide furniture to fill all rooms of the house at either a low cost or no cost. Major home-improvement companies that sell and repair appliances and other home repair and improvement-related services will have the opportunity to provide appliances at low cost or no cost.

ABOUT THE AUTHOR

Mr. Eric Lawrence Frazier, MBA
President & CEO, The Power Is Now Media

Mr. Eric Lawrence Frazier, MBA, is the President and CEO of The Power Is Now Media, a national multimedia company dedicated to real estate education, empowerment, and thought leadership. Through its expansive platform—The Power Is Now website (www.thepowerisnow.com), national podcast networks, social media channels, and live-stream television platforms—the company delivers timely, authoritative content on real estate, lending, economics, and government policy.

Publishing and Educational Contributions

As Publisher and Editor-in-Chief of The Power Is Now Publishing, Mr. Frazier oversees the production of books and magazines focused on real estate, financial literacy, and wealth building. Since its founding, the publishing division has developed The Power Is Now Magazines—a suite of online real estate publications launched in 2013 that offer market insights, national news, and educational resources for homebuyers and professionals.

Academic Background

Mr. Frazier holds both a Master of Business Administration (MBA) with an emphasis in Finance and a Bachelor of Science in Business Administration and Management from the University of Redlands, California.
He has lectured on the U.S. mortgage crisis at the University of California, Riverside, addressing international business leaders from India, and has also served as an adjunct professor.

Professional Expertise and Experience

With over four decades of experience in mortgage banking, Mr. Frazier is recognized nationally for his leadership in origination, underwriting, operations, management, and marketing.
He also holds a California real estate license for over thirty years and a broker's license (#01143484) for more than twenty-eight years.
Together with his wife, he founded Frazier Group Realty (www.fraziergrouprealty.com), a full-service, family-owned real estate company based in Riverside, California.

Spiritual Leadership

Mr. Frazier serves as a pastor and leads The Power Is Now Ministries, part of the North Fontana Church, a registered 501(c) nonprofit organization.
Through this ministry, he continues his mission of teaching, outreach, and mentorship.

Industry Leadership and Associations

Mr. Frazier's leadership extends across multiple professional associations. He has served as:

- President, Orange County Realtist chapter of the National Association of Real Estate Brokers (NAREB)
- Director, California Association of Real Estate Brokers
- Vice President, Orange County chapter of the National Association of Hispanic Real Estate Professionals (NAHREP)
- Advisory Board Member, Orange County chapter of the Asian Real Estate Association of America (AREAA)
- Board Member, Riverside Fair Housing Council
- He is also a current member of the Inland Valley Association of Realtors (IVAR).

Civic and Community Leadership

Beyond real estate, Mr. Frazier is committed to community service and education.
He has served on the Board of Directors of Project Tomorrow (www.tomorrow.org), a national nonprofit focused on advancing education.
He is an active member of:

- 100 Black Men of America
- NAACP
- National Association of Mortgage Brokers
- He is also a past President and Director of the State of California African American Museum (www.caamuseum.org).

Author, Speaker, and Creative Leader

A man of many talents, Mr. Frazier is also an author, blogger, poet, singer, songwriter, motivational speaker, business consultant, and coach for both for-profit and nonprofit organizations.
He has published six books on poetry, African American wealth, credit, and business.
His personal interests include golf, running, and jazz music.

Mentorship and Family Life

Mr. Frazier is deeply passionate about mentorship, serving as a role model for African American men and offering guidance to young people and adults alike.
His greatest joy is family—he has been married to Ruby, the love of his life, for over forty years. Together they have raised four accomplished daughters:

- Three hold master's degrees in management and business
- The youngest holds a bachelor's degree in apparel merchandising and management

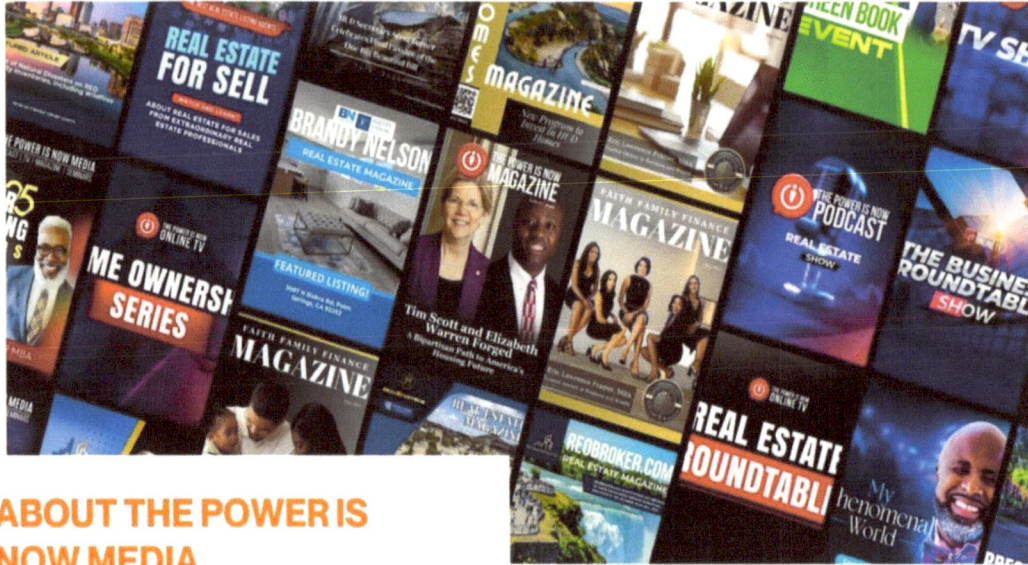

ABOUT THE POWER IS NOW MEDIA

Founded in 2009 by Eric L. Frazier, MBA, The Power Is Now Media is an online multimedia company headquartered in Riverside, California.

We are passionate advocates for homeownership, wealth building, and financial literacy.

Through our diverse platforms—including nationally syndicated radio, podcasts, magazines, TV, social media, streaming platforms, and live online seminars and webinars—we create and publish original educational content about real estate and financial empowerment.

As a trusted online platform and learning resource, we provide valuable information about homeownership, housing programs, loan options, and down payment assistance to help individuals and families achieve financial literacy and the American Dream of homeownership.

We are proudly supported by housing finance agencies, real estate associations, and civic, religious, and community organizations, helping them amplify their voice and promote their services and programs in lending, housing, and homeownership.

👉 Visit us online: www.thepowerisnow.com

Our Mission

The mission of The Power Is Now Media is to inspire and educate both consumers and real estate professionals to build wealth through real estate—from acquisition and management to sale.
We achieve this through our website, live and on-demand TV, and social media platforms, providing trusted information and tools that empower everyone to own real estate now and attain the American Dream of homeownership.

Company Slogan:

"We are leading the conversation about homeownership."

Address:
3739 6th Street, Riverside, CA 92501

Telephone/Fax:
800-401-8994

Founder & CEO:
Eric Lawrence Frazier, MBA

- **California Licensed Loan Originator (NMLS License #461807)**
- **California Real Estate Broker (License #01148434)**

WHY BECOME A MEMBER OF THE POWER IS NOW MEDIA?

Unlock exclusive access to the most powerful real estate, mortgage, credit, and wealth-building content in the industry.

For a limited time, become a member for only $10/month or $60/year. Your membership delivers undeniable value, insider access, and proven tools to help you buy, sell, invest, and build wealth with confidence.

Membership Benefits

Exclusive Streaming & Shows

· Unlimited access to The Power Is Now TV Network library of hundreds of shows, podcasts, and webinars.
· Daily programming on homeownership, real estate investing, mortgages, credit, and financial literacy.
· Member-only live streams and roundtable discussions with top industry leaders.

Free Digital Resources

- Real estate eBooks, guides, and reports on buying, selling, investing, and credit strategies.
- Buyer & Seller Guides, HUD Homes Guide, and Foreclosure Market Reports, updated quarterly.
- Access to The Power Is Now Media Resource Library of downloadable content.

Magazines & Newsletters

- Complimentary subscription to The Power Is Now National Real Estate Magazine.
- Complimentary subscription to The Power Is Now HUD Homes for Sale Magazine.
- Complimentary subscription to The Power Is Now TV Guide Magazine.
- Complimentary subscription to Faith, Family & Finance Magazine.
- Weekly newsletters with videos, infographics, and market insights.

AFRICAN AMERICAN HOMEOWNERSHIP INITIATIVE

THE POWER IS NOW MEDIA

Member Engagement

- Invitations to attend and participate in live recordings of the Real Estate Roundtable and Business Roundtable.
- Networking opportunities with agents, lenders, investors, and entrepreneurs nationwide.
- Priority access to quarterly webinars for first-time homebuyers, investors, and asset managers.
- Monthly group coaching sessions on Personal Finance, Real Estate, Mortgage, and Media.

Discounts & Savings

- Member-only discounts on media services (podcast hosting, YouTube TV production, private-label magazines, website redesigns, social media management).
- Exclusive pricing on advertising, sponsorships, and coaching programs.

Community & Recognition

- Become part of a national network of professionals and consumers committed to real estate wealth-building.
- Opportunities to feature your story, listings, or business on The Power Is Now TV Network.
- Special Membership Offer

JOIN NOW

Special Launch Price: $10/month or $60/year (limited-time offer through year-end).
Regular Price: $50/month or $325/year. Don't wait—membership pays for itself many times over.

www.ingramcontent.com/pod-product-compliance
Lightning Source LLC
Chambersburg PA
CBHW052053190326

41519CB00002BA/211